Teaching
Critical Thinking

bell hooks
the teaching trilogy:

More books by **bell hooks**
Available from Routledge

Teaching
Critical Thinking

Practical Wisdom

bell hooks

Routledge
Taylor & Francis Group

NEW YORK AND LONDON

First published 2010
by Routledge
711 Third Avenue, New York, NY 10017

Simultaneously published in the UK
by Routledge
2 Park Square, Milton Park, Abingdon, Oxon OX14 4RN

Routledge is an imprint of the Taylor & Francis Group, an informa business

© 2010 Taylor & Francis

Typeset in New Baskerville and Gill Sans by EvS Communication Networx, Inc.

Library of Congress Cataloging-in-Publication Data
Hooks, Bell.
Teaching critical thinking : practical wisdom / Bell Hooks.
p. cm.
Includes index.
1. Teaching. 2. Critical thinking. 3. Democracy and good governance. I. Title.
LB1025.3.H67 2009
370.15'2–dc22
2009016079

ISBN10: 0-415-96819-4 (hbk)
ISBN10: 0-415-96820-8 (pbk)
ISBN10: 0-203-86919-2 (ebk)

ISBN13: 978-0-415-96819-5 (hbk)
ISBN13: 978-0-415-96820-1 (pbk)
ISBN13: 978-0-203-86919-2 (ebk)

"Human existence, because it came into being through asking questions, is at the root of change in the world. There is a radical element to existence, which is the radical act of asking questions… At root human existence involves surprise, questioning and risk. And because of all this, it involves actions and change."

—Paulo Freire
Learning to Question:
A Pedagogy of Liberation

Contents

Teaching: Introduction

When I began my schooling in the all-black, segregated schools of Kentucky in the fifties I was lucky to be taught by African American teachers who were genuinely concerned that I, along with all their other pupils, acquired a "good education." To those teachers, a "good education" was not just one that would give us knowledge and prepare us for a vocation, it was also an education that would encourage an ongoing commitment to social justice, particularly to the struggle for racial equality. It was their strong belief that a teacher must always be humane. Their embodiment of both a superior intellect and an ethical morality shaped my sense of school as a place where the longing to know could be nurtured and grow. Teachers in our segregated schools expected us to attend college. They were infused with the spirit of W.E.B. DuBois, who proclaimed when writing about higher learning for black folk in 1933,

We hold the possible future in our hands but not by
wish and will, only by thought, plan, knowledge and
organization. If the college can pour into the coming age
an American Negro who knows himself and his plight
and how to protect himself and fight race prejudice, then
the world of our dream will come and not otherwise.

We were taught that education was the surest route to freedom.
The teachers were there to guide us, and show us the way to
freedom.

When I made my way to college, I was truly astonished to
find teachers who appeared to derive their primary pleasure
in the classroom by exercising their authoritarian power over
my fellow students, crushing our spirits, and dehumanizing our
minds and bodies. I had chosen to attend Stanford University,
a predominantly white college (primarily because the financial
aid packages were better than those offered by black institutions), but I never once considered what it would be like to
study with teachers who were racist. Even though I had attended a high school with outspokenly racist teachers who were con-
temptuous and unkind, I had romanticized college. I believed
it would be a paradise of learning where we would all be so busy
studying that we'd never have time for the petty things of this
world, especially not racism.

We need more autobiographical accounts of the first generation of black students to enter predominantly white schools,
colleges, and universities. Imagine what it is like to be taught by
a teacher who does not believe you are fully human. Imagine
what it is like to be taught by teachers who do believe that they
are racially superior, and who feel that they should not have to
lower themselves by teaching students whom they really believe
are incapable of learning.

Usually, we knew which white professors overtly hated us, and
we stayed away from their classes unless they were absolutely required. Since most of us came to college in the wake of a power-

ful anti-racist civil rights struggle, we knew we would find allies in the struggle, and we did. Remarkably, the outspoken sexism of my undergraduate male professors was even harsher than their covert racism.

Going to school in this strange new climate of racial change was both exhilarating and frightening. In those days, almost everyone was proclaiming the rise of a new age of equality and democratic education, but in reality the old hierarchies of race, class, and gender remained intact. And newly constructed rituals ensured they would be maintained. Trying to negotiate these two worlds—the one where we were free to study and learn like everyone else and the one where we were continually made aware that we were not like everyone else—made me a bit schizophrenic. I wanted to learn and I enjoyed learning, but I feared most of my teachers.

I went to college to become a teacher. Yet I had no desire to teach. I wanted to be a writer. I soon learned that working menial jobs for long hours did not a writer make and came to accept that teaching was the best profession a writer could have. By the time I finished graduate school I had encountered all types of teachers. Even though progressive teachers who educated for the practice of freedom were the exception, their presence inspired me. I knew that I wanted to follow their example and become a teacher who would help students become self-directed learners. That is the kind of teacher I became, influenced by the progressive women and men (black and white) who had shown me again and again, from grade school on into college, the power of knowledge. These teachers showed me that one could choose to educate for the practice of freedom.

Nurturing the self-development and self-actualization of students in the classroom, I soon learned to love teaching. I loved the students. I loved the classroom. I also found it profoundly disturbing that many of the abuses of power that I had experienced during my education were still commonplace, and I wanted to write about it.

When I first told my longtime editor at Routledge, Bill Germano, that I wanted to write a book of essays about teaching, he expressed concern. He said then that there may not be an audience for such a book, calling attention to the fact that I was not an education professor; my published work to date had focused on feminist theory and cultural criticism. I explained that in this new book I wanted to explore the connections between engaged pedagogy and issues of race, gender, and class, as well as the impact of Paulo Freire's work on my thinking. As he listened to me, which he always did, Germano was persuaded. And *Teaching to Transgress: Education as the Practice of Freedom* was published to much success in 1994.

Ten years later, I published *Teaching Community: A Pedagogy of Hope,* the "sequel" to *Teaching to Transgress* that continued to explore issues of engaged pedagogy. In the introduction, titled "Teaching and Living in Hope," I talk about the fact that the first teaching book reached an amazingly diverse audience, that it created a space for me to dialogue with teachers and students about education. I shared:

> In these past years I have spent more time teaching
> teachers and students about teaching than I have spent
> in the usual English Department, Feminist Studies, or
> African-American Studies classroom. It was not simply the
> power of *Teaching to Transgress* that opened up these new
> spaces for dialogue. It was also that as I went out into the
> public world I endeavored to bring as a teacher, passion,
> skill, and absolute grace to the art of teaching: It was
> clear to audiences that I practiced what I preached. That
> union of theory and praxis was a dynamic example for
> teachers seeking practical wisdom.

In the past twenty-plus years I have been asked to address many topics that were not covered specifically in the first two teaching books. I have been asked to comment on various issues, to answer questions that were deemed especially pressing for an individual teacher.

In this final book of the teaching trilogy, *Teaching Critical Thinking: Practical Wisdom*, I have not followed the previous two books' pattern of writing a collection of essays. Instead, in this book, I have highlighted issues and concerns that teachers and students placed before me and responded to each issue with a short commentary that I've called a "teaching." The thirty-two teachings discuss a wide range of issues, some simple and others complex. Issues of race, sex, and class are addressed from diverse standpoints. I was excited to write these short commentaries; there are so many worthwhile issues surrounding teaching that are worth considering, even if they do not invite a longer essay. A black woman professor wanted me to address how she could maintain authority in the classroom without being viewed through the lens of racialized sexist stereotypes as an "angry black woman." One teacher wanted me to talk about tears in the classroom, while another wanted me to talk about humor. It was particularly challenging to address the question of whether we can learn from thinkers and writers who are racist and sexist. The power of story, the essential role of conversation in the learning process, and the place of imagination in the classroom are just a few of the other subjects addressed in this collection.

All of the topics discussed in this book emerge from my conversations with teachers and students. While the topics are not connected by a central theme, they all emerge from our collective desire to understand how to make the classroom a place of fierce engagement and intense learning.

Teaching 1

Critical Thinking

On the cover of my memoir *Bone Black* there is a snapshot of me taken when I was three or four. I am holding a toy made in vacation Bible school, a book shaped like a dove. I often joke that this picture could be called "a portrait of the intellectual as a young girl"—my version of *The Thinker*. The girl in the snapshot is looking intensely at the object in her hands; her brow a study in intense concentration. Staring at this picture, I can see her thinking. I can see her mind at work.

Thinking is an action. For all aspiring intellectuals, thoughts are the laboratory where one goes to pose questions and find answers, and the place where visions of theory and praxis come together. The heartbeat of critical thinking is the longing to know—to understand how life works. Children are organically predisposed to be critical thinkers. Across the boundaries of race, class, gender, and circumstance, children come into the world of wonder and language consumed with a desire for knowledge. Sometimes they are so eager for knowledge that they become relentless interrogators—demanding to know the who, what, when, where, and why of life. Searching for answers, they learn almost instinctively how to think.

Sadly, children's passion for thinking often ends when they encounter a world that seeks to educate them for conformity and obedience only. Most children are taught early on that thinking is dangerous. Sadly, these children stop enjoying the process of thinking and start fearing the thinking mind. Whether in homes with parents who teach via a model of discipline and punish that it is better to choose obedience over self-awareness and self-determination, or in schools where independent thinking is not acceptable behavior, most children in our nation learn to suppress the memory of thinking as a passionate, pleasurable activity.

By the time most students enter college classrooms, they have come to dread thinking. Those students who do not dread thinking often come to classes assuming that thinking will not be necessary, that all they will need to do is consume information and regurgitate it at the appropriate moments. In traditional higher education settings, students find themselves yet again in a world where independent thinking is not encouraged. Fortunately, there are some classrooms in which individual professors aim to educate as the practice of freedom. In these settings, thinking, and most especially critical thinking, is what matters.

Students do not become critical thinkers overnight. First, they must learn to embrace the joy and power of thinking itself. Engaged pedagogy is a teaching strategy that aims to restore students' will to think, and their will to be fully self-actualized. The central focus of engaged pedagogy is to enable students to think critically. In his essay "Critical Thinking: Why Is It So Hard to Teach?" Daniel Willingham says critical thinking consists

> of seeing both sides of an issue, being open to new
> evidence that disconfirms young ideas, reasoning

dispassionately, demanding that claims be backed by evidence, deducing and inferring conclusions from available facts, solving problems, and so forth.

In simpler terms, critical thinking involves first discovering the who, what, when, where, and how of things—finding the answers to those eternal questions of the inquisitive child—and then utilizing that knowledge in a manner that enables you to determine what matters most. Educator Dennis Rader, author of *Teaching Redefined*, considers the capacity to determine "what is significant" central to the process of critical thinking. In their book *The Miniature Guide to Critical Thinking: Concepts and Tools*, Richard Paul and Linda Elder define critical thinking as "the art of analyzing and evaluating thinking with a view to improving it." They further define critical thinking as "self-directed, self-disciplined, self-monitored and self corrective." Thinking about thinking, or mindful thinking about ideas, is a necessary component of critical thinking. Paul and Elder remind us:

> Critical thinkers are clear as to the purpose at hand
> and the question at issue. They question information,
> conclusions and point of view. They strive to be clear,
> accurate, precise, and relevant. They seek to think beneath
> the surface, to be logical and fair. They apply these skills to
> their reading and writing as well as to their speaking and
> listening.

Critical thinking is an interactive process, one that demands participation on the part of teacher and students alike.

All of these definitions encompass the understanding that critical thinking requires discernment. It is a way of approaching ideas that aims to understand core, underlying truths, not simply that superficial truth that may be most obviously visible. One of the reasons deconstruction became such a rage in academic circles is that it urged people to think long, hard, and critically; to unpack; to move beneath the surface; to work for knowledge. While many critical thinkers may find intellectual or academic fulfillment doing this work, that does not mean that students have universally and unequivocally embraced learning to think critically.

In fact, most students resist the critical thinking process; they are more comfortable with learning that allows them to remain passive. Critical thinking requires all participants in the classroom process to be engaged. Professors who work diligently to teach critical thinking often become discouraged when students resist. Yet when the student does learn the skill of critical thinking (and it is usually the few and not the many who do learn) it is a truly rewarding experience for both parties. When I teach students to be critical thinkers, I hope to share by my example the pleasure of working with ideas, of thinking as an action.

Keeping an open mind is an essential requirement of critical thinking. I often talk about radical openness because it became clear to me, after years in academic settings, that it was far too easy to become attached to and protective of one's viewpoint, and to rule out other perspectives. So much academic training encourages teachers to assume that they must be "right" at all times. Instead, I propose that teachers must be open at all times, and we must be willing to acknowledge what we do not know. A radical commitment to openness maintains the integrity of the critical thinking process and its central role in education. This commitment requires much courage and imagination. In *From Critical Thinking to Argument* authors Sylvan Barnet and Hugo Bedau emphasize that, "Critical thinking requires us to use our imagination, seeing things from perspectives other than our own and envisioning the likely consequences of our position." Therefore, critical thinking does not simply place demands on students, it also requires teachers to show by example that learning in action means that not all of us can be right all the time, and that the shape of knowledge is constantly changing.

The most exciting aspect of critical thinking in the class-room is that it calls for initiative from everyone, actively inviting all students to think passionately and to share ideas in a passion-ate, open manner. When everyone in the classroom, teacher and students, recognizes that they are responsible for creating a learning community together, learning is at its most meaning-ful and useful. In such a community of learning there is no fail-ure. Everyone is participating and sharing whatever resource is needed at a given moment in time to ensure that we leave the classroom knowing that critical thinking empowers us.

Teaching 2

Democratic Education

Growing up in the fifties when schools were still racially segregated and the seeds of civil rights struggle were being spread quietly, folks talked about the meaning and value of democracy. It was both a public discourse and a private topic of conversation. Black men like my father who had fought in the all-black infantry during the second world war came home disillusioned by a nation that had sent them to fight and die to "keep the world safe for democracy" while denying them civil rights. This disillusionment did not lead them to despair. It served as the catalyst for them to struggle on the home front to make our nation truly democratic. Throughout my high school years, I participated in the Voice of Democracy essay contests put on as part of their scholarship programs. In my essays, I would passionately express my views that our country was a great nation, the greatest nation in the world, because the United States was committed to democracy. I wrote that all citizens needed to assume responsibility for protecting and maintaining democracy.

Like many black children, I had been taught that one of the most important aspects of our democracy was that it granted the right of education to everyone irrespective of race, gender, or class.

There is little public discourse among students today about the nature of democracy. Nowadays, most students simply assume that living in a democratic society is their birthright; they do not believe they must work to maintain democracy. They may not even associate democracy with the ideal of equality. In their minds, the enemies of democracy are always and only some foreign "other" waiting to attack and destroy democratic life. They do not read the American thinkers, past and present, who teach us the meaning of democracy. They do not read John Dewey. They do not know his powerful declaration that "democracy has to be born anew in each generation, and education is its midwife." Highlighting the need to align schooling with democratic values, James Beane and Michael Apple paraphrase John Dewey in their book *Democratic Schools* to explain, "If people are to secure and maintain a democratic way of life, they must have opportunities to learn what that way of life means and how it might be led." When disenfranchised groups of American citizens worked to change all educational institutions so that everyone would have equal access—black people/people of color and white females, along with allies in struggle—there was a dynamic national discourse about democratic values. In keeping with that discourse, educators were deemed crucial conveyers of democratic ideals. At the core of these ideals was a profound, ongoing commitment to social justice.

Many of those allies in struggle were white males who, by virtue of circumstance and privilege, had been at the forefront of efforts to make education a site where democratic ideals would always be realized. Yet, many of these proponents of democratic values were divided. In theory, they expressed the belief that everyone should have the right to learn and yet, in their practice, they helped maintain hierarchies within educational institutions wherein privileged groups were given advantage. Like Thomas Jefferson, who contributed much to the rise of democracy, their minds were divided. Although he could proclaim "educate and inform the mass of people," in much of his work Jefferson's split mind was revealed. On one hand he could speak and write eloquently about the need to uphold the spirit of democracy and of equality, and on the other hand he could own slaves and deny black people basic human rights. Despite these contradictions, Jefferson did not waver in his belief that embracing change was crucial to the "progress of the human mind." He wrote, "As that becomes more developed, more enlightened, as new discoveries are made, new truths discovered and manners and opinions change, with the change of circumstances, institutions must advance also to keep pace with the times." Certainly, as the critique of imperialist white-supremacist capitalist patriarchal values gained momentum, schooling and education began to undergo profound and radical changes.

Conservative dominator culture responded to these changes by attacking public policies like affirmative action that had provided the means by which institutions of higher learning could include disenfranchised groups. Consequently, the doors to education that had opened and allowed the disenfranchised to enter were closing. The subsequent rise of private schools undermined public schools, while teaching for testing reinforced discrimination and exclusion, and segregation on the basis of race and class has quickly become an accepted norm. On all fronts, funding for education has been cut. Progressive professors who had once pushed for radical change were simply bought off. High status and high salaries motivated them to join the very system they had once worked so hard to dismantle.

By the 1990s, Black Studies, Women's Studies, and Cultural Studies were all revamped so that they were no longer progressive locations within educational systems from which a public discourse about freedom and democracy could be vocalized. They were, for the most part, deradicalized. And in those loca-

tions where deradicalization did not take place, they were ghet-
toized, deemed a suitable playground for students who wanted
to assume a radical persona. Today, professors who refuse to
comply with deradicalization are often marginalized or even
encouraged to leave academia. Those of us who stay, who continue to work to educate for the practice of freedom, see firsthand the ways that democratic education is being undermined
as the interests of big business and corporate capitalism encourage students to see education solely as a means to achieve material success. Such thinking makes acquiring information more
important than gaining knowledge or learning how to think
critically.

The principle of equality, which is at the core of democratic
values, has very little meaning in a world in which a global oligarchy is taking over. Using the threat of terrorist attack to con-
vince citizens that free speech and protest place our nation at
risk, governments globally are integrating fascist policies that
undermine democracy on all fronts. Explaining that "capitalism no longer needs democracy" in his powerful polemic *How
the Rich Are Destroying the Earth*, Herve Kempf contends:

> Thus, democracy has become antithetical to the objectives
> the oligarchy seeks: democracy favors opposition to
> unwarranted privileges; it feeds doubts about illegitimate
> powers; it pushes for the rational examination of decisions.
> It is consequently more dangerous all the time during
> a period when the harmful tendencies of capitalism are
> becoming more obvious.

Now more than ever before in our nation, we need educators to make schools places where the conditions for democratic
consciousness can be established and flourish.

Educational systems have been the primary place in our nation where free speech, dissent, and pluralistic opinions are
valued in theory and practice. In her thoughtful consideration

of this subject, *Wrestling with the Angel of Democracy: On Being an American Citizen*, Susan Griffin reminds us that "to keep the spirit of democracy alive requires a continual revolution." In her profound meditation on democracy, *The Healing of America*, Marianne Williamson emphasizes ways that the democratic principle of unity in diversity remains the foundation of democratic values:

> There are people in America who overemphasize our unity yet fail to appreciate the importance of our diversity, just as there are those who emphasize our diversity yet fail to appreciate the importance of our unity. It is imperative that we honor both. It is our unity and our diversity that matter, and their relationship to each other reflects a philosophical and political truth outside of which we cannot thrive.

Griffin echoes these sentiments: "In a democracy many different points of view about every possible subject will be expressed, and almost all of them must be tolerated. This is one reason why democratic societies are usually pluralistic." The future of democratic education will be determined by the extent to which democratic values can triumph over the spirit of oligarchy that seeks to silence diverse voices, prohibit free speech, and deny citizens access to education.

Progressive educators continue to honor education as the practice of freedom because we understand that democracy thrives in an environment where learning is valued, where the ability to think is the mark of responsible citizenship, where free speech and the will to dissent is accepted and encouraged. Griffin contends that,

> those who would contribute to democratic consciousness would transgress the boundaries of prejudice and assumption is consistent with the deep desire for free

speech and thought, not just as tools in the eternal battles
for political power that occur in every era but from an
even more fundamental democratic impulse, the desire to
enlarge consciousness.

Democratic education is based on the assumption that democracy works, that it is the foundation of all genuine teaching
and learning.

Teaching 3

Engaged Pedagogy

Engaged pedagogy begins with the assumption that we learn best when there is an interactive relationship between student and teacher. As leaders and facilitators, teachers must discover what the students know and what they need to know. This discovery happens only if teachers are willing to engage students beyond a surface level. As teachers, we can create a climate for optimal learning if we understand the level of emotional awareness and emotional intelligence in the classroom. That means we need to take time to assess who we are teaching. When I first began work in the classroom, like many teachers I was most concerned, if not a bit obsessed, with whether or not a substantive amount of information and assigned material was covered. To make sure we had time in the classroom to cover the material that I believed really mattered, I did not take the time to ask students to introduce themselves or to share a bit of information about where they were coming from and what their hopes and dreams might be. I noticed, though, that when I did make time for everyone to get acquainted, the classroom energy was more positive and more conducive to learning.

Knowing all that I know now after more than thirty years in classrooms, I do not begin to teach in any setting without first laying the foundation for building community in the classroom. To do this it is essential that teacher and students take time to get to know one another. That process can begin by simply hearing each person's voice as they state their name. When I first encountered Vietnamese Buddhist monk Thich Nhat Hanh I was awed by his insistence that when a student is in the presence of a powerful, insightful teacher much can be learned even before words are spoken. He explains: "The Chinese say, 'When a sage is born, the water in the river and in the plants and trees on the mountains nearby became clearer and more green.'" Even though Thay (Nhat Hanh) is speaking about a spiritual teacher, those of us who have been in classrooms with incredible professors know that their presence illuminates.

When we see the classroom as a place where teacher and students can share their "inner light" then we have a way to glimpse who we are and how we might learn together. I like to engage the minds and hearts of students by doing simple writing exercises, sentence completions. We might all write a spontaneous paragraph beginning with a phrase like "my most courageous moment happened when…." Or we might bring a small object to class and all write a short paragraph about its value and importance. Reading these short paragraphs aloud to one another, we have the opportunity to see and hear each unique voice. Most professors know what it is like to sit in a classroom of twenty or more students, where you wish for scintillating dialogue and only the same two or three students talk. Writing and reading paragraphs together acknowledges the power of each student's voice and creates the space for everyone to speak when they have meaningful comments to make.

I never ask students to do an in class writing assignment that I am not willing to do. My willingness to share, to put my thoughts and ideas out there, attests to the importance of putting thoughts out there, of moving past fear or shame. When we all take risks, we participate mutually in the work of creating a learning community. We discover together that we can be vulnerable in the space of shared learning, that we can take risks. Engaged pedagogy emphasizes mutual participation because it is the movement of ideas, exchanged by everyone, that forges a meaningful working relationship between everyone in the classroom. This process helps establish the integrity of the teacher, while simultaneously encouraging students to work with integrity.

The root meaning of the word "integrity" is wholeness. Hence, engaged pedagogy makes the classroom a place where wholeness is welcomed and students can be honest, even radically open. They can name their fears, voice their resistance to thinking, speak out, and they can also fully celebrate the moments where everything clicks and collective learning is taking place. Whenever genuine learning is happening the conditions for self-actualization are in place, even when that is not a goal of our teaching process. Because engaged pedagogy highlights the importance of independent thinking and each student finding his or her unique voice, this recognition is usually empowering for students. This is especially important for students who otherwise may not have felt that they were "worthy," that they had anything of value to contribute.

Engaged pedagogy assumes that every student has a valuable contribution to make to the learning process. However, it does not assume that all voices should be heard all the time or that all voices should occupy the same amount of time. Early on in my graduate career and in the first years of teaching, I had been a student in classes where teachers were almost obsessively concerned with "fairness." To them, this meant that every student should be given the same amount of time to speak and that every voice should have equal substantive weight. Often, this led to circumstances where students who were not prepared would talk on and on. In the engaged classroom students learn the value of speaking and of dialogue, and they also learn to speak when they have something meaningful to contribute. Understanding that every student has a valuable contribution to offer to a learning community means that we honor all capabilities, not solely the ability to speak. Students who excel in active listening also contribute much to the formation of community. This is also true of students who may not speak often but when they speak (sometimes only when reading required writing) the significance of what they have to say far exceeds those of other students who may always openly discuss ideas. And of course there are times when an active silence, one that includes pausing to think before one speaks, adds much to classroom dynamics.

When students are fully engaged, professors no longer assume the sole leadership role in the classroom. Instead, the classroom functions more like a cooperative where everyone contributes to make sure all resources are being used, to ensure the optimal learning well-being of everyone. Ultimately, all professors want students to learn, and to see education as a means of self-development and self-actualization. In *Teaching to Transgress: Education as the Practice of Freedom,* I state: "To educate for freedom, then, we have to challenge and change the way everyone thinks about pedagogical process. This is especially true for students." Engaged pedagogy is vital to any rethinking of education because it holds the promise of full participation on the part of students. Engaged pedagogy establishes a mutual relationship between teacher and students that nurtures the growth of both parties, creating an atmosphere of trust and commitment that is always present when genuine learning happens. Expanding both heart and mind, engaged pedagogy makes us better learners because it asks us to embrace and explore the practice of knowing together, to see intelligence as a resource that can strengthen our common good.

Teaching 4

Decolonization

Critical pedagogy encompasses all the areas of study that aim to redress biases that have informed ways of teaching and knowing in our society ever since the first public school opened. The two great movements for social justice in our nation that both changed all aspects of our culture and created small but powerful revolutions in education are the civil rights and feminist movements. After the militant push for racial equality led to desegregation and the changing of laws, black power activists were one of the first groups in this nation to call attention to all the myriad ways education was structured to reinforce white supremacy, teaching white children ideologies of dominance and black children ideologies of subordination. For example, they critiqued school children being taught that "Columbus discovered America" (a bias that denied the presence of indigenous native people in this nation before colonizing whites came to the so-called new world), and they exposed the knowledge that

African explorers had traveled to this soil before Europeans. Few people in our nation of any race want to remember the way in which black power activists worked in public schools both to see that children who were hungry would be fed and to offer them what Malcolm X called "new ways of seeing" themselves and the world.

Concurrently, feminist challenges to patriarchy and its concomitant insistence on the primacy of male thinkers and their works was an insurrection that created major changes. When a critique of race and class was added to that of gender, every bias was interrogated. To progressive teachers and students this was truly a revolution, making it possible for many of us to enter areas of study that were previously seen as arenas available solely to privileged white males. Many of us attended colleges and universities that would not have enrolled us had there not been both movements for equality aimed at redressing race, sex, and class biases and a movement for reparations and reconstruction (misnamed as "affirmative action"). It was as though the use of the word "affirmative" deemed that a big "yes" was being bestowed on the underprivileged by the privileged, hence it reinscribed the very structure of paternalistic domination that it was meant to redress. That aside, it did make it possible for many people from exploited, oppressed, and/or disenfranchised classes to seek higher education just at a historical moment where imperialist white-supremacist capitalist patriarchy was being questioned on an international front and here at home.

Drawing from the radicalism of militant freedom fighters from Africa, South America, China, and all over the world, radicalized Americans, especially those from disenfranchised groups, were learning a new language with which to articulate our place in the United States. Albert Memmi explored the relationship between the "colonizer and the colonized" and Frantz Fanon looked toward decolonization. Walter Rodney showed us "how Europe underdeveloped Africa." Léopold

Sédar Senghor gave us "negritude" and Amílcar Cabral spoke of the "decolonizing of mentality." Everyone was reading Marx. Some folks were working to put together race, gender, and class so that we could truly examine our world from an understanding of the way that difference articulated itself politically in our daily lives.

"Liberation" was a term constantly evoked. And it was incredibly liberating to learn a more complex political language with which to name and understand the politics of our nation. It was incredibly liberating to move past notions of personal prejudices and hatreds to look at systems of domination and how they operated interdependently. The most essential lesson for everyone, irrespective of our race, class, or gender, was learning the role education played as a tool of colonization here in the United States. Of course critics of this term, especially when applied to the experience of African Americans, insisted that it was inappropriately used because we were not indigenous inhabitants of a country we owned, with a distinct language and culture. They refused to acknowledge the link between the political fate of black citizens of the United States and black folks on the African continent.

Significantly, progressive black folks here talked most about the colonization of the mind. That colonization began for Native peoples, for black, brown, and yellow people with the assumption that our history here began with the civilizing presence of the colonizer. In *Pedagogy in Process: The Letters to Guinea-Bissau*, Paulo Freire contends:

> The culture of the colonized was a reflection of their
> barbaric way of seeing the world. Culture belonged only
> to the colonizers. The alienating experience of colonial
> education was only counteracted for the colonized at
> those moments when, in an urge for independence, they
> rejected some of its aspects.

For many first-generation-to-attend-college black people/ people of color, the seeds planted that led us to reject a coloniz- ing mentality were sowed within us prior to entering institutions because we could not have been ready to receive the "gifts" of affirmative action had we not already learned to resist passive acceptance of the pressures of dominator values and perspec- tives on our identity. Usually we learned a measure of resistance to dominant culture within our homes. That spirit served us well in educational institutions where we faced an onslaught of biased dominator thinking.

Without a decolonizing mentality, smart students from dis- enfranchised backgrounds often find it difficult to succeed in the educational institutions of dominator culture. This holds true even for those students who have embraced the values of dominant culture. In fact, those students may be the least pre- pared for the barriers they face because they have so convinced themselves that they are different from other members of their group. A major flaw in all of our nation's powerful move- ments for social justice has been and remains the assumption that liberation will take place in one fell swoop. That has been detrimental to progress simply because once certain gains in the direction of equality were achieved, the struggle stopped. And, of course, that is dangerous when one is attempting to construct sub-cultures of self-determination within the frame- work of dominator culture. We would all have fared better in our struggles to end racism, sexism, and class exploitation if we had learned that liberation is an ongoing process. We are bombarded daily by a colonizing mentality (few of us manage to escape the received messages coming from every area of our lives), one that not only shapes consciousness and actions but also provides material rewards for submission and acquiescence that far exceed any material gains for resistance, so we must be constantly engaging new ways of thinking and being. We must be critically vigilant. This is no easy task when most people spend most of their days working within dominator culture.

Those of us who work in education have been particularly fortunate because, individually, we are able to work against reinforcing dominator culture and biases with little or no resistance. College professors have tremendous freedom in the classroom. Our major difficulty is sharing knowledge from an unbiased and/or decolonized standpoint with students who are so deeply mired in dominator culture that they are not open to learning new ways of thinking and knowing. Recently, I gave a lecture wherein a young white female student boldly stated during open discussion: "I am one of those evil capitalists you critique and I do not want to be changed by participation in your classroom or reading your books." After I called attention to the fact that the word "evil" was not used during my lecture or in any work referred to, I was able to share that in all the classes I teach I make it clear from the start that my intent is not to create clones of myself. Boldly, I affirmed: "My primary intent as a teacher is to create an open learning community where students are able to learn how to be critical thinkers able to understand and respond to the material we are studying together." I added that it has been my experience that as students become critical thinkers they often of their own free will change perspectives; only they know whether that is for the better.

Since there has not been a radical transformation of education at its roots, education as the practice of freedom is still a pedagogy accepted only by individuals who elect to concentrate their efforts in this direction. We deliberately choose to teach in ways that further the interest of democracy, of justice. Since the radical interventions in education that have helped end many discriminatory practices, thereby creating diverse contexts for unbiased learning, have been severely attacked by dominator culture their impact is diminished. Concurrently, many "radical" thinkers often speak radical theory and then engage in conventional practice sanctioned by dominator culture. Certainly, rewards received by the dominant educational hierarchy diminish efforts to resist and transform education. Understanding that liberation is an ongoing process, we must pursue all opportunities to decolonize our minds and the minds of our students. Despite severe setbacks, there have been and will continue to be constructive radical shifts in the way we teach and learn as minds "stayed on freedom" teach to transgress and transform.

Teaching 5

Integrity

Throughout the history of education in the United States, both in the public school system and in higher education, imperialist capitalist white-supremacist patriarchal politics has shaped learning communities, affecting both the way knowledge has been presented to students and the nature of that information. It has only been in the last twenty years that there has been radical questioning of what we teach and how we teach it. Education as a tool of colonization that serves to teach students allegiance to the status quo has been so much the accepted norm that no blame can be attributed to the huge body of educators who simply taught as they were taught. When even a small child can question "If the Native American Indians were here before Columbus then how could Columbus have discovered America?" there must have always been teachers who questioned, who saw clearly that much of what they taught was aimed at reinforcing the politics of imperialist white-supremacist capitalist patriarchy.

By forcing education to be the tool of mass colonization, dominator culture basically made the classroom a place without integrity. Not all learning was biased in the direction of the status quo, but most of it was, especially in grade schools. Having been taught to believe in the superiority of empire, of the United States, of whiteness, and of maleness, by the time most grade school students reached college their indoctrination had deep roots. One of the great revolutions of the last fifty years has been the questioning of biases by educators. Much of that questioning began in the sixties when militant black power advocates interrogated the way in which the teaching of history and literature was distorted to ensure that black folks would have internalized self-hatred. From the fifties on, civil rights struggle had led aware black folks to question how we were taught about ourselves, about black history. In many black homes, parents told their children different narratives of our history and our past from those learned from white-supremacist teachers. In my early high school years, I can remember asking my teachers why we never read any literature by black writers. I was told that there were no black writers. When I came to school with a list of black writers my parents had given me, I was told their writing was not "great" literature, that it was inferior and not worthy of being taught. In those days, no one in the educational system questioned the way in which white-supremacist thinking informed teaching.

Even though most teachers, especially white teachers, were just following the rules, teaching as they had been taught, the dishonesty and the hateful biases informing their teaching were profoundly damaging to all students. Gender discrimination, supported most intimately by religious teachings in our lives growing up, was reinforced both in our schools and in our homes. Whereas racist thinking was more often than not challenged by our parents, most parents did not intervene and challenge the information their children received at school. Clearly, internalized racist thinking informs the way a majority of black folks teach and parent. And most black people have been colonized, taught to accept and uphold white supremacy. Black people who would march for civil rights protesting white racism might in their homes uphold aesthetic white supremacy, teaching their children to value light skin and to devalue dark skin. Much of this internalized racism was fostered and nurtured in educational settings.

Racism is just one of the systems of domination that has been perpetuated and maintained by educators. Just as I was told in high school that there were no black writers, I was taught in my undergraduate years at an elite college that women could not be "great" writers. Fortunately, I had one white woman professor who taught us to recognize patriarchal biases and challenge them. Without her counter-hegemonic input, how many females would have had their longing to write crushed, would have graduated thinking why try if you can never be good enough?

Whatever the emphasis in dominator culture (sexism, racism, homophobia, etc.), until very recently almost all teachers played a major role in enforcing, promoting, and maintaining biases. Therefore, most classrooms were not a setting where students were taught in such a manner that the values of honesty and integrity were at the core of learning. And despite interventions, many classrooms have not changed. Classrooms cannot change if professors are unwilling to admit that to teach without biases requires that most of us learn anew, that we become students again. At the college where I teach, a white male sociology professor took pride in the fact that he would tell students at the onset that in his course the focus would be on class and not on race and gender. Presumably, he meant that like old leftists he would simply focus on economics as he was trained to do. Maybe he did not want students to examine the myriad ways race and gender inform the construction of class in our society. Or it could be that, with typical white-supremacist and patriarchal thinking, he was confident that race and gender really did not affect class relations. His authoritarian announcement effectively silenced students from even raising questions.

We will never know the full extent to which the betrayal of integrity through bias in education has been and continues to be psychologically damaging. Contemporary critiques of biases as they inform education, how we learn what we learn, have been the radical intervention that has made it possible to restore integrity to the classroom. Integrity is present when there is congruence or agreement between what we think, say, and do. The root meaning of the word has to do with wholeness. In *The Six Pillars of Self-Esteem* Nathaniel Branden defines the term: "Integrity is the integration of ideals, conviction, standards, beliefs—and behavior. When our behavior is congruent with our professed values, when ideals and practice match, we have integrity." There is little or no discussion of integrity in the classroom. Unfortunately, many teachers and students think of integrity as an old-fashioned concept that has little meaning in a world where everyone is striving for success And yet, when students learn in a context without integrity it is likely that they will internalize what psychoanalyst Alice Miller calls "poisonous pedagogy."

At all educational institutions today there are teachers who have responded constructively to the critique of biases by changing their curriculum and choosing to teach in a manner that honors the diversity of our world and our students. These teachers, who recognize that their classrooms must be places where integrity is valued for education as the practice of freedom to become the norm, are courageous because the world all around them devalues integrity. Choosing to maintain high standards for pedagogical engagement and performance is one way to ensure that integrity will prevail.

Teaching 6

Purpose

In the larger society, the world beyond academic settings, everyday folk are concerned with the issue of purpose. They want to have a clearer understanding of life, of what gives life meaning. In professional settings, teachers, especially those of us who work at the college and university level, rarely discuss our sense of purpose. We rarely talk about how we see our role as teachers. To a grave extent, my understanding of a teacher's role was defined by knowledge received from the teachers I had observed as a student. Teachers seemed to fall into three categories: those who saw teaching as an easy job with long vacations, those who saw teaching as solely about the transmitting of information and knowledge that could be easily measured, and finally those who were committed to expanding the intelligence of their students—to helping students learn more. It was this third category of teachers who influenced me the most, and who continue to influence and inspire me.

They were the teachers who were concerned with the integration of thinking and learning information. They were the committed teachers who wanted to see students grow and self-actualize. There was the grade school teacher who recognized that I loved to read and allowed me to check out more books from the library than was deemed appropriate, and there was the college professor who passed out copies of a poem I had written with no name attached to see if the gender of the writer could be identified. In that short exercise she proved to all of us in her classroom that gender did not determine whether or not one could be a good writer. By showing us the falseness of sexist thinking, common at the time, which insisted females could never write work that was as good as the work of male writers, she tore down prison walls that had colonized our imaginations and held our minds captive. This was a life-changing transforming moment for me.

I had arrived at Stanford University from a small, segregated world in Kentucky but whether in all-black schools or in the racially integrated high school I attended, I had always been told that I was a good writer. When I arrived at college, professors constantly interrogated me about my writing, suggesting that I was either helped by someone else or maybe even guilty of passing off the words of another. Even though these questions were usually answered to the teacher's satisfaction, they were a powerful blow to my self-esteem. Writing in the class of Diane Middlebrook, the acclaimed author of critical work on Anne Sexton and Sylvia Plath, the wounds to my creative spirit were mended. She affirmed that I had a strong and powerful writing voice and that I would grow and mature as a writer. These are the teaching moments that inspired me. In just a few classes, she challenged all her students to think beyond sexism. In her classroom, we were changed.

Despite stellar moments like this, mostly I found the classroom a dehumanizing place as a student. It was the painful experiences that motivated me to strive to teach in ways that were humanizing, that would lift my students' spirits so that they would soar toward their own unique fullness of thought and being. Even though I had a clearly defined purpose as a teacher, I did not understand at the beginning of my teaching career that the majority of students would arrive in the classroom colonized in their minds and imaginations. I was unprepared for the reality that many teachers would view with hostility the idea of education as the practice of freedom. At the start of my teaching career, I had not learned skills that would enable me to facilitate the opening of closed minds.

Even though I saw humanization, the creation of a learning community in the classroom, as my purpose, and recognized that in order to fulfill this task I would need to teach critical thinking, when students began to "change" their minds as a consequence of study in our classrooms, I felt concerned that I was transcending appropriate boundaries. In my untenured years, I felt tremendous stress about efforts to teach in ways that differed from the norm. Always there was a fear of punishment. And the worst fear was the failure to reach a student, to be attacked and assailed on all sides by students. Professors who strive to educate as the practice of freedom are most inclined to resist their own purpose when there is a student or a group of students who constantly disrupts class with negative questioning. When students responded to my practice with negativity (even if it was only a small, vocal group of students who did so), I felt extreme self-doubt. It was the individual successes, akin to my own experience in Middlebrook's class, which restored my faith and kept me from faltering.

Teaching 7

Collaboration

(written with Ron Scapp)

Collaborating with diverse thinkers to work toward a greater understanding of the dynamics of race, gender, and class is essential for those of us who want to move beyond one-dimensional ways of thinking, being, and living. My collaboration with philosopher Ron Scapp is one of the relationships of solidarity both in friendship and intellectual endeavor that enables us to have a more expansive view of the world and the culture we live within. Both Ron and I see our teaching as always connected to struggles for social justice. We have relied on one another for support, critique, and innovation in our life and work. We turn toward one another for critical feedback, whether it is a discussion of the role of imagination in teaching or more personal decisions like career changes and the struggle to stay with the right livelihood.

Both Ron and I believe that it is through dialogue that we best struggle for clearer understanding of dominator culture and the particular dynamics of race, gender, class, and sexuality which emerge. Our ongoing dialogue repeats and expresses what we do in the classroom. It is a constant effort to sustain critical consciousness about what we do, how we do it, and why. Linking our academic positions to social justice both in and outside the classroom has meant that we exist in a liminal space within the academy; we both belong and are simultaneously outsiders to academia. So much of what we do is constantly seen as suspect and interrogated by those in power who are more invested in the status quo.

At a time when many people refer to a need for dialogue, especially dialogue that promotes diversity, we seek to ensure that there is a link between theory and practice. All too often we find in academic circles that colleagues do little more than pay lip service to the hard work involved in maintaining the type of connection that requires ongoing radical openness and commitment to change. To remain critically vigilant, Ron and I engage a philosophical approach to dialogue. What this means is that we deploy the strategies of dialectical exchange, which emphasizes considering and reconsidering one's position, strategies, and values. Even though Ron and I have worked with ideas in collaboration for almost twenty years, we still occupy very different locations within the hierarchies of race, class, and gender. This has given us an opportunity to move across boundaries and push past the obstacles which ordinarily preclude intimate intellectual bonding across differences. Both of us are frequently "called out" by the other person; asked to stand back and engage in rigorous self-critique; to look realistically at the ways we inhabit a different world. Concurrently, we also identify what we share that is common to us.

Despite much that is dated in his discourses of critical pedagogy, Paulo Freire continues to serve as a guide for our progressive efforts to redefine education as the practice of freedom. In *Learning to Question: A Pedagogy of Liberation*, he reminds us that when we step outside the constraints of our individual daily life and enter into diverse cultural spaces and standpoints, we must always be ready to "give honest answers" to questions that typically prevent mutual understanding across difference from emerging. In our conversation in *Teaching Community: A Pedagogy of Hope* we emphasized the importance of establishing and maintaining trust, which means understanding that what is essential to us is creating a dialogue between our differences that enriches us both.

We continually focus on the issue of trust because the most common complaint we hear from people of color about whether they feel able and willing to strive for solidarity across differences is their fear that white people cannot be trusted, especially privileged white males. And it is equally true that racist conditioning has socialized many white people to be suspicious of people of color, especially when we refuse to stay confined within the limits of racist notions of self and identity. What Ron and I have learned in the constant re-evaluation and re-affirmation of our bond is that trust is not static, that it must be constantly re-enforced by the actions we are willing to take both to own the importance of our bond and to protect it.

In Ron's work, he is often challenged by skeptical individuals who feel he is not living out the commitment to ending domination that he professes in his published collaborations with me. What they fail to understand is that there is not a singular map for how we enter struggles to educate for freedom. Our collaborative effort to challenge and embrace each other is an ongoing expression of critical resistance yet it must necessarily reflect our differences, the unique locations we inhabit. And it will necessarily assume different forms. Ron continues to work at an institution in a major large city, while I have relocated and work at a small Christian need-based college in my home state of Kentucky. While Ron has continually worked to subvert the privileges that could easily be his within imperialist white-supremacist patriarchy by using his power in a manner that actually undermines structures of domination, he never pretends that there are not slippages and moments where he continues to benefit from the very system he critiques. This is why our collaborative project of ongoing critical thinking together is crucial as we strive to maintain our commitment to working for freedom for everyone and, as we struggle to maintain integrity within systems that do not value dissenting voices.

My career choices have led me further and further away from full-time college teaching. Yet, every major vocational decision I have made has been seriously examined by the two of us. Frequently, because of Ron's position on race and gender privilege (he has worked within institutions as a high level administrator), he often understands better how the system works and also what can be done to subvert it. Without my comradeship with Ron, I might not have remained in the university. At my darkest hours, when I felt systematically attacked within academic institutions, when I believed that my only hope of sane survival was to leave the academy, Ron set forth the arguments for why it was important for me to continue teaching. He highlighted the ways my presence is as much a teaching tool as the work because it embodies the practices of engaged pedagogy. He is ever ready to call attention to the positive way students and teachers apply my work, the ways it acts as an intervention affirming what Freire calls the effort we must make to "maintain hope even when the harshness of reality may suggest the opposite." Concurrently, Ron is much more likely to enter academic environments where he could compromise his integrity and receive more positive attention and reward. His efforts to maintain radical commitment are constantly buttressed by our critical dialogue and by the constant engagement with progressive students who challenge and critique him.

Our mutual dialogue is both public and private. Our effort has been to translate our vision of solidarity into reality so that we can provide a model to everyone that solidarity across difference is not only possible but necessary. We see that teachers and students look at what we have done and what we do as witness and testimony. It is a concrete indication of all that is possible as we put in place the anti-racist, anti-sexist paradigms that can transform all our lives and provide us with hope that a different future is possible. We believe that the critical pedagogy we have enacted has been a small part of the cultural revolution that has made it possible for an African American to become President of this struggling democracy. Ron's willingness to engage in useful collaboration also serves as a model for the way in which critical thinkers represent a voice for change. Envisioning a future of global peace and justice, we must all realize that collaboration is the practice that will most effectively enable everyone to dialogue together, to create a new language of community and mutual partnership.

Teaching 8

Conversation

Engaged pedagogy produces self-directed learners, teachers, and students who are able to participate fully in the production of ideas. As teachers, our role is to take our students on the adventure of critical thinking. Learning and talking together, we break with the notion that our experience of gaining knowledge is private, individualistic, and competitive. By choosing and fostering dialogue, we engage mutually in a learning partnership. In most classrooms, teachers present the material and students passively receive it. They either commit to memory what the teacher says or take notes to remind them. Most students rarely read these notes once a class has ended. Having successfully regurgitated the material, they feel no need to hold onto the knowledge once it has been used to meet the material demands of the course. In retrospect, when I consider my undergraduate years what I remember most is not the energy and content of presentations, but rather the conversations generated by class discussion.

Much knowledge acquisition comes to us in daily life through conversations. As a teaching tool, both in and outside the classroom, conversation is awesomely democratic. Everyone talks, everyone engages in conversation. In *Learning Redefined* Dennis Rader extols the power of conversation: "Conversation contains dialogue, the exchange of understandings and meanings in the endeavor to construct between information. Conversation is always inclusive; it encourages and nourishes individual voice as it strives to develop a community of vision." Across race, class, and gender, everyone engages in conversation. And everyone remembers a good conversation where the back-and-forth sharing of ideas enhanced our understanding, the sharing of wit and wisdom stimulated our capacity to think critically and allowed us to engage in dialectical exchange.

Much of the teaching that I currently do begins with the large lecture. Even though I agree to give lectures, I see the monologue as the least useful tool for the transmission of ideas. Since most audiences lack the skills of active listening, much information offered in lectures is missed. And I often find that what is not missed is misunderstood. The future of learning lies with the cultivation of conversations, of dialogue. I agree with Rader that "conversations bring out the wit in others while presentations merely display the wit, or lack of it, of the presenters." Most importantly, talking with teachers and students about how and when the most ecstatic moments of learning occur, I hear again and again the primacy of conversation.

Those of us who recognize the value of conversation as a key to knowledge acquisition also know that we are living in a culture in which many people lack the basic skills of communication because they spend most of their time being passive consumers of information. Both television and computers help promote passive learning. Much feminist theory that critically examines constructions of masculinity shows that to make boys into patriarchal men, society trains them to value silence over speech. They may find themselves becoming people who either cannot talk or, when they talk, can only engage in a monologue. These are the people who talk at us, who by refusing to converse, promote and maintain a hierarchy of domination wherein withholding gives one power over another person. Conversation is always about giving. Genuine conversation is about the sharing of power and knowledge; it is fundamentally a cooperative enterprise.

In a group conversation with Paulo Freire more than thirty years ago, I heard him state emphatically that "we cannot enter the struggle as objects in order to later become subjects." This statement resonated with my being. It affirmed for me the importance of finding and having a voice. To speak, to be able to name was a way to claim the subject position. Many students often feel that they have no voice, that they have nothing to say that is worthy of being heard. This is why conversation becomes such a vital intervention, for it not only makes room for every voice, it also presupposes that all voices can be heard.

A conversation-based model of learning is especially useful when a classroom is diverse. We have all been, to some extent, socialized to feel comfortable listening in on or talking in a conversational manner, so defensive barriers are less likely to be put up. In classroom discussions that are not conversations there is often a sense that argument and negative contestation are the only ways to address relevant issues. Negative conflict-based discussion almost always invites the mind to close, while conversation as a mode of interaction calls us to open our mind. All too often, professors have feared that if a conversation begins in the classroom that it will foreclose discussion of assigned reading material, of what matters, at least to them. However, mindful conversation, talking that is powerful and energetic, always spotlights what *really* matters. When conversations in the classroom lead to intense dialogue, students bring a heightened awareness to their engagement with assigned material. Rader believes that "Conversation—true conversation—is the way we cleanse poisons, such as false assumption, prejudices, ignorance, misinformation, lack of perspective, lack of imagination, and stubbornness from the system." While it is not productive to engage in negative dialogues when the intent is more to win an argument than to share ideas, conversations that teach us may be loud and energetic; they may be fierce. In her book *Fierce Conversations: Achieving Success at Work and in Life, One Conversation at a Time* author Susan Scott urges us to reconsider the word "fierce," explaining that "in Roget's Thesaurus...the word fierce has the following synonyms: robust, intense, strong, powerful, passionate, eager, unbridled, uncurbed, untamed." Such a conversation can be a learning experience and fun. It can be a location where knowledge acquired stays with us, empowering us to abandon fear and insecurity and find the place of compassion and connection. Compassion creates a spirit of tolerance; it intensifies the longing to communicate, to understand.

Rader insists that conversation promotes understanding, which he sees as a "different kind of knowing, one that is more aware of the whole and its interactive variables." Explaining further he shares this insight:

> Conversations are powerful. They can turn us toward
> different definitions and different pathways. They help us
> look at complicated matters from different perspectives
> as we turn them this way and that while striving to
> construct a new understanding.

Conversations are not one-dimensional; they always confront us with different ways of seeing and knowing. According to Rader, they generate "engagement and contribution."

Many of the ideas in this essay and in this book were talked about in conversations between me and educator Dennis Rader. When I felt my internal thought processes were not as energetic as I wanted them to be, I would talk with Dennis and feel renewed energy. Writing this short essay, I began to worry that it was impossible to discern where my thoughts ended and his began. This made me think again about the democratic nature of conversational learning. There is much obsession in academic circles about the ownership of ideas. Competition for academic regard leads individuals to have a desperate need to be seen as the "one" who first thought of an idea. In reality, ideas are always circulating. They are made new as we engage in internal critical reflection, internal conversations that give fresh expression to common thought.

In the workshops on teaching that I facilitate in classroom discussions, ways of knowing expressed in conversations are what draw listeners in and provide them with intellectual nourishment. Much of what we remember, what stays with us, emerged in conversations. It is my hope that future educators will talk more and more, together and with students, so that the model of conversation as a way to learn will have its rightful place as a genuine location for serious and rigorous thought.

Teaching 9

Telling the Story

Telling stories is one of the ways that we can begin the process of building community, whether inside or outside the classroom. We can share both true accounts and fictional stories in a class that help us understand one another. For years, I was hesitant to share personal stories. I had been trained to believe that anyone who relied on a personal story as evidence upholding or affirming an idea could never really be a scholar and/or an intellectual, according to dominator thinking via schools of higher learning. Telling a personal story to document or frame an argument was a sign that one was not dealing in hard facts, that one was not scientific enough. I am grateful to have lived long enough to learn how much information we have been given and told was hard science or data was really a story, the interpretation of data and facts. When the information received, most especially in hard science, countered the data once held to be immutable fact, the story changed. I am grateful to have lived to see a moment in cultural history where we know via science about our brain and how it processes information, about the stories it tells and allows us to tell. In *The Story Factor: Inspiration, Influence, and Persuasion through the Art of Storytelling* Annette Simmons expresses it this way :

> Stories are "more true" than facts because stories are
> multidimensional. Truth with a capital "T" has many
> layers. Truths like justice or integrity are too complex
> to be expressed in a law, a statistic, or a fact. Facts need
> the context of when, who, and where to become Truths.
> A story incorporates when and who—lasting minutes or
> generations and narrating an event or series of events
> with characters, action and consequences. It occurs in a
> place or places that gives us a where.

Stories enchant and seduce because of their magical multidimensionality.

I have told many stories about my childhood, whether writing memoirs, feminist theory, or about race and class. I have used fragments of memories, and at times huge chunks, as a catalyst for critical essays, cultural criticism, and books for children. In every book I published, there is a sibling reader who is eager to remind me that what I am describing never really happened, or it did not happen the way I am describing it. This occurs even though I have shared that there is no absolute truth, that we all believe what we see from our perspective, and that the individual perspective is always limited.

Remembering stories is such an essential tool for thinkers and writers. Rather than assuming, "I think therefore I am," I like to think I am because the story is. The stories I tell about who I am constitute the me of me-as-I-see-it as I tell it. For me, stories infuse writing with an intimacy that often is not there when there is just plain theory. Everyone who reads my work in its entirety knows that early on there were very few, if any, personal stories in the work. However, I began to realize that if I wanted to write theory, especially feminist theory that would be read across the boundaries of race, gender, class, and educational levels, I would need to provide a common entry point. I have written elsewhere about the many times early on in my career where I spoke with audiences whom I had been told were not interested in "theory," only to find that if I prepared them for a shift in paradigms by telling a story to illustrate critical points, my ideas would be received with greater openness. This changed the nature of my writing. It also changed my life.

For in writing various stories about the me of me and telling those stories in books and in therapy sessions, my wounded spirit began to heal. The soul murder I felt as a child was no longer the mark of my being; by telling stories I had entered a redemptive space. I had entered a world of soul retrieval. Slowly, I was taking the broken bits and pieces of my psyche and putting them together again, creating in the process new and different stories—liberating tales. Lyrics from a song we sing in the traditional black church give definition to this change: "My soul looks back and wonders—how I got over." This song is about survival and triumph; it joyously heralds the sense of wonder that arises when we move past trauma and find ourselves whole again.

Transformations in my process of self-actualization and growth changed my work in the classroom, as well. Finding that stories helped students to think critically, I shared my stories and encouraged students to share their own stories. We used spontaneous writing of paragraphs, which we then read aloud to another. This exercise allows us to hear each individual story and it also gives us an opportunity to hear each person's voice. Active listening draws us closer together. Students listen to one another's stories with an intensity that is not always present during a lecture or class discussion. One of the ways we become a learning community is by sharing and receiving one another's stories; it is a ritual of communion that opens our minds and hearts. Sharing in ways that help us connect, we come to know each other better. Dennis Rader describes the way in which stories help us engage the complexities of conflict and paradox: "Story provides the framework for contextual awareness. When we know the story, we see and comprehend the previously hidden or misinterpreted.... Stories can excite, inform, expand, and parameter conversation.... Stories provide a sense of community, a cohering feeling of shared concerns, values, and investigations." They become the sparks that ignite a deeper passion for learning.

Stories also help us heal. In many ways, when folks seek a therapist much of what takes place is the telling of stories. A therapist may listen to a client's stories and endeavor to show connections between past and present as a way to nourish healing. In the classroom, we link our stories to assigned material, using them to illuminate this work. Bringing emotional intelligence to the telling of stories heightens our awareness and perception.

Here is one of my favorite stories, a story that teaches and helps me. This is my version; there are many ways this story can be told. A student seeking to understand better the process of self-actualization goes to the teacher and says, "I often suffer from a split mind, a lack of congruence between what I think, say, and do. How can I end this suffering?" The teacher tells the student that the potential for this split is happening inside everyone. For inside all of us there is a "sick self and a self struggling to be well and they are in conflict." When the student asks the teacher which self is winning the conflict, the teacher replies "whichever self you feed." I hear this story as a reminder that we have a choice not only about how we perceive reality, but also how we create reality. I hear it telling me that I can determine my reality by both the choices I make and all that I imagine, think, and believe. There are days when I feel lost and find I can return to mindful awareness by telling this story and challenging myself to identify what part of me I am feeding.

Stories help us to connect to a world beyond the self. In telling our stories we make connections with other stories. Journeying to countries where we may not speak the native tongue, most of us communicate by creating a story, one we may tell without words. We may show by gesture what we mean. What becomes evident is that in the global community life is sustained by stories. A powerful way we connect with a diverse world is by listening to the different stories we are told. These stories are a way of knowing. Therefore, they contain both power and the art of possibility. We need more stories.

Teaching 10

Sharing the Story

Academic classrooms were fundamentally changed by contemporary feminist movement's insistence that "the personal is political," that experience is to be valued as much as factual information, and that there is indeed a place in the learning process for telling one's personal story. In the worst case scenario, in some classrooms confessing became the central basis for class discussion. In those classrooms, assigned reading would often be ignored as students talked with one another about their personal stories. These were extremely rare settings. However, individuals who oppose any use of personal experience in the classroom have often made critiques suggesting that any use of experience in learning meant that a class was no longer academic or that such a class could not be seen as engaging students in intellectual work. This is simply not the case.

In all classrooms, even in the hard sciences, professors use stories, usually in the form of anecdotes, to illustrate points,

to elucidate information that may be abstract. Story, especially
personal story, is one of those powerful ways to educate, to create community in a classroom. This is especially true as classrooms have become more diverse. At one time colleges and
universities had a population of mainly middle- and upper-class
white folks, mostly males. Classrooms were more homogenous
and students were, to some extent, already familiar with one
another's personal stories. When classrooms are more diverse,
there is simply a greater likelihood that conflict and contestation will happen. The more diverse a classroom, the greater the
likelihood that there will be different levels of knowing and as
a consequence professors cannot rely on a shared knowledge
base to build community.

When students learn about one another through the sharing of experience, a foundation for learning in community can
emerge. It is always the task of teachers to ensure that using
experience as a learning tool does not usurp assigned reading.
Usually, through paragraph writing that relates to assignments,
I encourage students to share personal experience by reading
what they have written to their classmates. Reading a short paragraph does not take as much time as spontaneous moments of
personal confession. When I learn more about students, I know
better how to serve them in my role as teacher.

In all cases when I ask students to write personal paragraphs
either in response to sentence endings or to a question, I also
write a paragraph. It is important to a learning community to
dismantle unnecessary hierarchies. Let me be clear here. As
long as an individual professor is the only person who evaluates
the work of students and grades, our status in the classroom
is never that of equals. However, this does not mean that professors must be authoritarian or lord it over students. It does
mean that we teachers must always be willing to acknowledge
our power in the classroom. We should not engage in false notions that all our voices carry equal weight. When professors
courageously share personal experience in a manner that illu-

minates assigned material, we help lay the foundation for building an authentic learning community. By making ourselves vulnerable we show our students that they can take risks, that they can be vulnerable, that they can have confidence that their thoughts, their ideas will be given appropriate consideration and respect.

When everyone in a classroom, including the teachers, shares personal experiences, the uniqueness of each voice is heard. Even when two people write and speak about common experiences, there is always a unique aspect, some detail that separates one experience from the other. Of course students must learn, if they do not already have the skill, how to integrate and use personal confession as a means to learn more about assigned material. When this skill is lacking, personal confession can simply become a form of exhibitionism, or even a competition where students actively compete to be the one telling the best or most memorable story. Clearly, when sharing personal experience is perceived by students as a way to derail the class and move away from assigned reading material, usually because a student or students have not done required work, it interferes with learning. Competition in the classroom diminishes everyone. It reduces learning to spectacle, requiring that some students be mere passive observers while other students dominate classroom discussion.

One of the most common complaints I hear from professors about their classrooms is the difficulty they face when students simply will not talk. Students often are afraid they will be shamed by teachers and/or peers. Unfortunately, this happens especially in classrooms where teachers claim that they want to hear students talk, but in actuality they dread having to listen to students. An aspect of that dread is just the simple fear that students will speak about concerns and issues that the professor may feel unable to address. When students are offered the opportunity to engage in discussions that either focus on or include discussion of personal experience, they are more able and willing to speak out. As stated earlier, I am passionate about writing short paragraphs which students read in class because this exercise allows everyone's voice to be heard and usually lays the groundwork for more engaging classroom discussion of assigned reading.

Hearing one another's personal experience in the classroom promotes an atmosphere of cooperation and deep listening. Ultimately, the negative possibilities that can arise when teachers validate the sharing of personal experience are small compared to the positive rewards when such sharing helps create a community of learning and enhances ways of knowing.

Teaching 11

Imagination

Teachers rarely talk about the role imagination plays in helping to create and sustain the engaged classroom. Since much of the work in a given course is the sharing of facts and information it is easy to discount the role of imagination. And yet what we cannot imagine cannot come into being. We need imagination to illuminate those spaces not covered by data, facts, and proven information. In Dennis Rader's unpublished manuscript *Learning Redefined* he argues that educators must shift their thinking about what constitutes learning, that it is vital for us to understand that cultivating the imagination depends on initiative. He calls attention to educators who remind us that facts are energized by the imagination. He quotes George David Miller who shares this insight in his work *Negotiating Toward Truth*:

> Educators who value imagination have little problem
> affirming creativity and dynamism. Imagination points

us beyond routine and static possibilities. But more
than throwing us toward such possibilities, imagination
synthesizes. It connects those things that were
previously disconnected. Syntheses are creative acts. They
represent the creation or births of new pathways, new
possibilities, new hopes, and new dreams.

And yet imagination receives so little attention.

Writer Toni Morrison made a visit to a school for gifted
children and while she found them extremely technologically
advanced (they knew everything about computers), she discovered in talking with them that they lacked imagination. Overall
in our culture the hours spent gazing at the television set seems
to stop creative processes. We live in a world where small children are encouraged to imagine, to draw, paint pictures, create
imaginary friends, new identities, go wherever the mind takes
them. Then, as the child begins to grow, imagination is seen
as dangerous, a force that could possibly impede knowledge
acquisition. The higher one goes up the ladder of learning, the
more one is asked to forget about imagination (unless a creative path has been chosen, the study of art, filmmaking, etc.)
and focus on the information that really matters. J. B. Priestley
contends:

> Because most children are highly imaginative, it is
> supposed by some that to reach maturity we ought to
> leave imagination behind, like the habit of smearing our
> faces with chocolate. But an adult in whom imagination
> has withered is mentally lame and lopsided, in danger of
> turning into a zombie or a murderer.

In dominator culture the killing off of the imagination serves
as a way to repress and contain everyone within the limits of the
status quo.

Listening to students talk about the myriad ways that they

feel diminished when teachers refuse to acknowledge their presence or extend to them basic courtesy in the classroom, I am continually awed by our power as teachers to help or hurt our students, to bolster their spirits or break them. Movements for social justice (anti-racist, feminism, gay rights) all insisted on acknowledgment of the way in which the personal is political. In the ongoing critique of dominator culture, thinkers and/or activists dedicated to changing society so that everyone can have equal access to basic human rights called attention to the "colonization" of the mind and imagination. They emphasized the various ways individuals from oppressed and/or exploited groups had been socialized to be self-hating and as a consequence could not begin to grow and become responsible citizens without first undergoing a shift in consciousness. This shift usually required folks to learn how to think outside the box. To think outside the box we have to engage our imaginations in new and different ways.

Imagination is one of the most powerful modes of resistance that oppressed and exploited folks can and do use. In traumatic circumstances, it is imagination that can provide a survival lifeline. Children survive abuse often through imagining a world where they will find safety. Within white-supremacist culture, black folks began a "black is beautiful" movement to resist the continual onslaught of negative representations of blackness. Without the ability to imagine, people remain stuck, unable to move into a place of power and possibility. Although Rosamund Stone Zander and Benjamin Zander do not use the word "imagination" often in their book, *The Art of Possibility: Transforming Professional and Personal Life*, the expansive engaged pedagogies they describe can only happen when triggered by creative imagination. In their introduction "Launching the Journey" they claim:

> Our premise is that many of the circumstances that
> seem to block us in our daily lives may only appear to

do so based on a framework of assumptions we carry
with us. Draw a different frame around the same set
of circumstances and new pathways come into view....
Revolutionary shifts in the operational structures of our
world seem to call for new definitions of who we are and
what we are here for.

Essentially they are talking about thinking outside the box.

Although Zander and Zander do not use the word "imagination" that often, they do testify that without pressing concerns
for survival "a person stands in the great space of possibility in
a posture of openness, with an unfettered imagination for what
can be." When a teacher lets loose an unfettered imagination in
the classroom, the space for transformative learning is expanded. We bring imagination into our work by thinking of new and
different ways to engage the particular group of students we
are teaching at a given moment in time. When I teach African
American literature and give the students an assignment to go
out into the world and read the poetry of Langston Hughes to
strangers and then write about their impressions and responses,
I am imagining that they will have a different experience recit-
ing and/or reading a poem aloud and witnessing its impact on
a listener than they would reading quietly to themselves in the
safety of private rooms or libraries.

No matter the subject I am teaching, I always use the writing and reading of spontaneously written paragraphs to stir our
collective imagination in the classroom. When we are free to let
our minds roam it is far more likely that our imaginations will
provide the creative energy that will lead us to new thought and
more engaging ways of knowing.

Teaching 12

To Lecture or Not

Big lecture halls filled with an audience of willing listeners no longer terrify me, but the large lecture is not the site I would choose for teaching. I am at my best teaching in the smaller workshop setting, where it is possible to get acquainted with the folks I am speaking to and with. I make it through giving a lecture by imagining I am sitting in a living room talking with a small group of people. I think of a lecture as the appetizer before the main meal. The question and answer session is the main moment for me because it is the moment of participatory engagement—the moment when I am no longer speaking alone. Even though it is usually much shorter than the featured lecture presentation, it has a much greater chance of being the moment where we come together as a learning community.

Yet my heart is often pierced with terror during the question and answer period. I fear the possibility of failure—not being able to give a good enough response. I fear saying the "wrong" thing. I fear making comments that will alienate rather than unite, comments that push us apart rather than comments that bring us together in a shared act of learning. Genuine learning, like love, is always mutual. In any engaged dialogue where learning is taking place between teacher and student, lecturer and audience, both parties are giving and receiving. What they give and what they learn are not the same. Whenever I finish a lecture, I offer a word of thanks to individuals in the audience who have been especially attentive; their rapt listening heightens my engagement in what I am saying and inspires me to work harder to make my ideas clear and engaging. Their "silent" gift renews my spirit, especially if I am tired or not feeling well.

Talking for more than twenty minutes usually means that a good portion of the audience has ceased to listen, that their minds have wandered off, away from the speaker toward all that really matters in their life. Rarely is a lecture what matters. Yet I have been told by many folk that I have given a talk wherein something that was said helped them change the direction of their thinking and their life practice in a constructive way. Since I am not confident that the large lecture is the optimal space for learning I always appreciate such feedback.

When we as a culture begin to be serious about teaching and learning, the large lecture will no longer occupy the prominent space that it has held for years. For in many ways the lecture is the teaching moment that most promotes passivity and discourages participation from learners. Listeners often take notes, but I know of very few people who read these notes to learn from them once the lecture is over. Studying my own notes that I have taken during lectures, I often find that they convey little of what the speaker had shared. Of course, this may simply be a reflection of my skill as a note taker. My notes convey more about my mood of the moment. Needless to say, past a certain point that mood is often one of extreme irritability, usually because the speaker is going on and on, making no connection with an audience, not even an imaginary one.

A few weeks ago I attended a lecture on the subject of the mandala given by a white male scholar whose field is Asian Studies with a particular focus on Buddhism. The talk lasted for almost two hours. When it began, his audience, filled with many students, was engaged, animated, and attentive. But after the first fifty minutes of listening to a very fast talk, we were restless, eager for the question and answer period to wake us all up. I have always pondered the reasons a speaker gives an excessively long talk. Sometimes it just seems to be hubris about knowledge, a desire to show off all that one knows. Other times, the long-windedness and forgetfulness about time is generated by anxiety and fear. I once gave a standing-room-only lecture at a liberal arts college in Portland. Trying hard to abide by the invitation to speak for fifty minutes, I spoke for what felt like an eternity to me. I had been looking at my watch. And while my written text did not take more than forty minutes to read, I began to improvise to make sure I was filling the requirements for time. Now and then I would look at my watch to make sure I was not speaking too long. Then I noticed that many people were leaving. Taking a closer look at my watch, I saw that it had stopped. When an audience member told me the time, I was most embarrassed that I had talked on and on and on.

Many of my listeners, especially the young, found the long-windedness exhilarating. Afterwards, when I apologized for my excessive speech, I was told that it was a compelling marathon of a talk, like a rave or poetry jam that just goes on and on into the night as the speaker gets more jazzed. It may have been cheap entertainment; however, I am confident that it would have been hard for anyone to learn much from my speech that evening, even though I worked hard to redeem myself during the question and answer session. Audiences who really do not want to be participants prefer the kind of talk that becomes a performance, akin to a concert, where you groove with the sound but do not need to make an effort to really understand what is being said. The talk then becomes a place of spectacle. I can recall encouraging my Oberlin students to attend a talk by scholar and activist Angela Davis. They reported that it was "great," talking mostly about the energy of the crowd, the repeated standing ovations. When I asked them to share with me and each other what they had learned they had difficulty responding.

Like most professors who give frequent large lectures, I notice that I am (like my colleagues) much less likely to run on in marathon style if I have a text in front of me. The Buddhist scholar, on the other hand, had too many papers, so he ignored them, or shuffled them about trying to reconnect with points he wanted to emphasize. His talk was notably repetitive. Along the way he had forgotten the reason for the talk was not simply to display knowledge and information, but rather to teach us. To teach in the setting of a large lecture, one has to work harder to make connection with listeners. This is especially the case in settings where the lights are dim and speaker and audience cannot see one another. The audience can be lulled into a passive trance where they listen but do not hear.

The worst scenario that happens during the question and answer session is when the person the speaker has noticed nodding-off through much of the talk is the first to rush up to the microphone. This is the moment most speakers dread. Academic decorum and bourgeois manners dictate that politeness prevail (as it should), and that speakers act as though no matter what is said, it should be treated as valuable. This is a mistake. I have found it useful to let the audience know that if someone comes to the microphone and does their version of a marathon question, I will interrupt them, with loving kindness. This is no easy feat, no matter the degree of love or kindness. The other challenge is to remember not to feel compelled to respond to every question. My training in academic traditions of public speaking taught me to always answer questions even if I did not know the answer; and if I did not know the answer, to act as if I did. What a horrid teaching practice! For me it is best to be truthful, to state that I do not know an answer or that I will give thought to the question and respond to it later in another format. Academics fear confessing that we do not have the "answer" because we are afraid that audiences will shame us, or worse, see us as not very smart. When one adds race, gender, and class into the equation it becomes all the more risky to be perceived as not worthy, not good.

My most passionate critique of the large lecture format as we know it is that listeners often project into the talk material that I did not say. If a lecture was only fifteen to twenty minutes then there would be an abundance of time for speaker and listener to critically engage one another, to revisit points where there may be misunderstanding or projection. Now that listeners often "report" online what they are certain they "heard," it is even more likely that misunderstandings will occur and that words will be put into a speaker's mouth that were never chosen or used by the speaker.

It is my hope that there will be significant movement away from the all-encompassing large lecture. Jokingly, I often state that when I rule the academic world there will be no long, late night talks, no extended receptions, and no room for meaningless small talk. Given that there are not that many people of color/black people on the lecture circuit, more than other groups we are often expected to address all possible issues. Because an institution may have only one or two speakers who are not white in the course of a year, it is often all the more likely that these speakers will find it is assumed that every topic should be commented on. One of the negative aspects of looking for the one speaker of color/black speaker is that we are often asked to speak on the basis of skin color and not on the basis of interest in our work. There are even times when I hear testimony that a potential black speaker "drones" on and the push will still be to invite that person because it will "look bad" not to have diversity on one's speaker list. Well, there are plenty of interesting and compelling black speakers out there; it may just take a bit more effort to find them.

The best benefit of the large lecture is that it brings new readers to one's work. Listeners who come up after the talk sometimes share that they have never heard of you or your writing, "but," they say, "listening to you talk, I want to know more." Then, one way to think of the lecture is that it is a moment of preparation for learning that will take place somewhere else, at another time, away from performance and spectacle.

Teaching 13

Humor in the Classroom

Being smart and being serious are traits that teachers value. However, we can become so serious that we leave no place for humor in the classroom. Like many academics and/or intellectuals, I did not grow up thinking that humor was important. Instead, all through high school I was known for being serious. Much of my seriousness was a psychological response to unhappiness in our dysfunctional household. No one we encountered at school, student or teacher, was allowed to influence us, because our patriarchal-tyrannical caring parents believed only they should have the power of influence. It was always a struggle to navigate the space between the rules of home and the knowledge at school; trying to figure out what to keep from parents and what to share produced a split mind. Fundamentally, it made it hard to let go and experience pleasure at home or school.

More than anyone realizes, the students seen as nerds or geeks, students who are often gifted at book learning, carry the residue of pain and trauma. Many of us are simply emotionally numb, shut down, disassociated. I was not a fun girl at school or at college. Laughter, humor in general, was associated in my mind with letting go. My biggest goal in life during high school and undergraduate college years was not to let go, but to hold on—to keep a hold on life. Very little appeared "funny" to me, and almost nothing was worthy of laughter.

When I entered graduate school, it became all the more necessary for me not to be seen as a fun girl. Striving for success in the world of sexist academia, a male-dominated environment where female students were told every day by professors that we were not really as good as men, made it all the more important to appear serious. It was important to be perceived as capable of doing academic work. When race and class was added to the equation, for a black female it was all the more vital to adopt a persona of seriousness. Throughout my college years friends and colleagues would often let me know that they would "sure like to see you drunk or stoned" because they believed I was too serious, that I could have more fun if I just lightened up a bit.

Before I learned to laugh, to appreciate the power of humor, I learned that it was acceptable to be witty, especially if you were one of the wear-black-all-the-time, deconstructivist, radical, feminist-bitchy-diva girls who could give a harsh read (i.e., critique) or throw shade (add sarcasm and maybe even just a bit of contempt to one's critique). Your "cold, biting" response, especially if it was witty, could actually generate a laugh from listeners now and then. It was more fun to be seen as cool than to be caught enjoying healthy laughter. Wit is a mode of expression that shows keen, swift perception and it is intended to amuse. Using verbal skill, wit often fails to arouse laughter because more often than not listeners just "don't get it." I was once one of those individuals who could never tell a joke properly (it always came out like a convoluted exegesis) or get a joke (i.e., understand the punch line). I was one of those people who usually had to have the joke explained to me.

Beginning a career in teaching, especially assuming an assistant professorship in the English department of an Ivy League university, I found myself in an atmosphere of absolute seriousness in the classroom, a seriousness among the students that was often hiding anxiety and fear of not measuring up. It was not that my students feared failure. Most of them were all too aware of their academic intelligence; their underlying fear was that someone, anyone, might prove to be more intelligent. In this uptight atmosphere, I first tried to inject a few witticisms into the classroom. There was no laughter in response; in fact, there was not even a look of wry amusement. Rather than give up on my attempts to bring a bit of amusement into the classroom, I began to tell students after I offered a witty comment, "by the way, that was supposed to be funny." Ah, humor! It was my failed attempt to amuse that actually generated laughter. Understanding this, while continuing my ongoing search for effective teaching strategies, sometimes I would come to my class and apologize that I was not yet capable of being funny. I would say to students, "I am witty—you just don't get it—try harder." They began to laugh now and then. They began to understand wit.

My efforts at humor were usually supported by the many drama queens who signed up for my courses. One day, I arrived late for class (students coming late often were the recipients of my witty remarks). A favorite student of mine, a tall black male with a dancer's body, RuPaul-like in every way, with the exception of dress, was at the front of the class mimicking me, throwing shade and making everyone laugh. I joined in the laughter, and it was one of many moments of illumination that can happen in the classroom. I realized then that both wit and regular old everyday humor could really serve to create a more open atmosphere in the classroom. Simply put, laughter shared can draw groups closer together. This is especially true in classrooms where there is much that separates, where diversity is the norm, or where the subjects studied confront students with depressing facts.

Classes where students are learning new ways of thinking and knowing that may challenge all the belief systems they have heretofore held dear need humor as a mediating force. Classes where students are being taught to confront dominator culture and its concomitant racism, sexism, class elitism, religious fundamentalism, homophobia, etc., can both depress the spirit and awaken feelings of powerlessness. When major differences of identity, experience, thought, and opinion are evident, tension and conflict can and does erupt in the classroom. Humor can provide a needed break from serious, intense material and discussion.

Attempts at humor can often be misunderstood, sometimes what we hope will amuse will instead create tension. Currently I teach at a college where a large majority of the staff, teachers, and students are committed to social justice, to all the big important issues that must be confronted if we are to end domination in all its forms. It is also a Christian college. Of all the places I have taught, it is a location where there is just not enough humor. Individuals are often so concerned that they not hurt anyone's feelings that forms of self-censorship emerge. My first year of teaching I invited Ron, a white male professor, a New York colleague and collaborator, to come and engage in a faculty workshop where we would have a conversation about teaching. Our time was limited; we had an hour to talk together. After introductions, Ron began to talk. And talk he did. He went on and on, as though he was the sole presenter giving a lecture. I stood by feeling confused and annoyed. Finally, I interrupted him and offered what I hoped would be amusing commentary saying "white men can ramble," making reference to the movie *White Men Can't Jump*. Even though some participants laughed, faculty later expressed concern that I was rude to our guest. After making my witty comment, I stated that Ron clearly had a lot to say and we were certainly willing to listen, but I thought it important to state that we were not having a dialogue.

Now, I could have interrupted Ron and stated just that, saying: "Ron, you are giving a long monologue when our purpose was to engage in a dialogue. I do not understand why you are doing this." That direct confrontation seemed more inappropriate to the occasion than a humorous comment. Later, when Ron and I made time for critical feedback about the presentation, he acknowledged that he just "got carried away." He had a lot to say and he wanted to say it. Well, how many times in the academic world do white males use the power of their voice to silence the voices of people of color—way too many. I felt Ron needed to examine whether or not he felt in competition with me and whether he sought to win the competition by making it impossible for my words to be heard, since there was so little time left for me to speak. After much difficult discussion we laughed together, and Ron admitted "white men can ramble."

Despite the fact that we had been engaged in conversations about pedagogy for years, it was not easy for us to engage in this critical dialogue. Frankly, I was "pissed" at Ron. I felt he had made a mockery of what was to have been an occasion for faculty to see a white male professor dialogue in a mutual way with a black female. It had been my hope that our interaction would serve as a model. It was a fiasco. Later, I was critiqued by faculty members for not being courteous to our guest. They missed the point. My response to Ron's hogging the limelight was to offer a witty critique of race and gender politics. Who in academe has not been faced with a similar situation—compelled to listen to a white male go on and on and on. While it is indicative of both our commitments to ending racism and sexism that Ron and I discussed our perceptions of the event, what took place, articulating critique, we are rarely angry with one another. It would have been easier for us both to just let the moment pass rather than to engage in critical feedback acknowledging the presence of hostility. Our ability to laugh together once we constructively addressed the issues so that we both felt we learned from what took place, created a bridge, reminding us both that what connects us and brings us together is always more valuable than the conflicts that may cause us to feel estranged or separate from one another.

Fear of conflict often leads teachers and students to refuse direct confrontation of issues when they may serve as useful teaching moments. Most of the white and black women who were present at the workshop Ron and I facilitated were encouraged by my willingness to speak out about the way he was using the moment to grandstand. We all know that it is not easy for women to confront men in most circumstances where there are major power differences. Fundamentally, humor helped create an atmosphere where we could talk about what happened within the group and with one another.

Talking with public school teachers, college professors, and students, I found that everyone agreed on the importance of humor in the classroom. My sister G. who teaches in an impoverished area at an inner-city school often finds that she has to be a stern disciplinarian. She was surprised when her students called attention to the fact that she never laughed in class. She realized that she withheld her humor and laughter for fear of losing power and authority, for fear of losing control. When she began to allow her funny self to emerge, she felt like she was more vulnerable, but the students appreciated this vulnerability and the sense of openness that shared laughter can bring. Concurrently, when we shift our minds into laughter we move from the left brain to the right brain creating a whole new place for thinking and dreaming, for creating great ideas.

I hope future efforts by educators to redefine learning will include discussions of ways to use humor productively in the classroom. We all know the kinds of negative humor that estrange people from one another, especially humor that relies on contempt to trash another person or group (i.e., humor that bashes people of color and white women, even if members of that group among the ones doing the dirty talk). We are not as familiar with the healing power of humor. When humor is used to wound or hurt by either a teacher or students, it is the responsibility of everyone in the classroom to find ways to acknowledge what has happened and to work at mending the tear in the class body politic. All teachers could use more studies about sharing the power of humor as a force in the classroom that enhances learning and helps to create and sustain bonds of community. Working together in the classroom, teachers and students find equanimity when we laugh together.

Teaching 14

Crying Time

There is always the risk of a student breaking into tears when confronting difficult subject matter in the classroom that is intimately connected to "real life." In the classrooms of many black professors, that tearful student is usually a white female. Indeed, a black female feminist colleague asked me to address this issue, hostilely referring to it as the "crying white girl syndrome." Tears surface so often in the classroom when the racial dynamics of white and black are being discussed because so much shame and guilt emerges; there is not an emotional distance when the issue is race that there may be with other less loaded topics.

More than thirty years ago, when I began teaching novels by black women writers, there would invariably be an intense emotional response to the fiction we were reading that led to tears from white and black female students. Black females often wept because reading a particular novel was the first public discourse where the pain of internalized racism as it affects the self-esteem of young black girls was given a voice. Certainly, this is what Toni Morrison has stated was the catalyst for her writing her first novel *The Bluest Eye*, the recognition that at least at that time there were few fictions that placed the stories of little black girls at the center. White female students who had never known that there was a color caste system among black folks, or if they knew had never realized fully its impact on the body and being of black children, wept because they were overwhelmed by the narration of their pain.

Some professors see the tears of white girls as a bid for attention or as a distraction that derails class discussion. There are times when this is so, whether that is the intention of a student or not. Importantly, when there is a weeping student, it is the teacher who must discern if those tears can be used to nurture a deeper class discussion or if they are an intrusion. The best way to discern this is to get to know one's students, to observe from the very first class the different ways that individuals are responding. Sometimes factors outside the classroom are causing grief and words stated in the classroom may simply trigger those emotions.

During the deep unhappiness of my teenage years I would often find myself in a late afternoon history class weeping quietly. All around me, students and teacher pretended not to notice. The high school had only recently been desegregated. To achieve that end black students were forced to rise earlier than usual and go by bus to the "white" school where we would be herded into the gym and compelled to wait for the white students to arrive and enter the school first. White supremacist logic held that this was the way to keep the peace. Despite the presence of the National Guard and fully armed white policemen with guns, integration had taken place without incident and it was vital to the administrators that no racial incident should occur. No wonder, then, that in an all-white classroom, with only two other black students present, no one wanted to acknowledge my feelings, my grief.

When the teachers discussed my emotional collapse they must have related it to home life. My therapist once asked me whether this class took place right before it was time for me to return home. And yet no one wanted to confront that domain. Melancholy, suicidal, whatever my emotional state, they deemed it better to ignore it. Since I pondered suicide often, I imagined the conversation they would have if I actually killed myself. Would anyone talk about the many times I sat in the classroom seemingly overwhelmed by grief. At home, I was known for my endless crying. My six siblings did not cry. Shaming me, they nicknamed me after the actress Jean Autry, known for playing the role of the "poor little rich girl" who often dissolved into passionate fits of weeping. By the time I reached graduate school my tears had stopped, my grief had been laid aside, covered up by an intense anger toward dominator culture and the folks who kept it all neatly in place.

When I began to teach, the memories of my tears and the way in which they were simply ignored were triggered when students in my class would respond to readings or discussions with passionate tears. I did not want to discount the emotions of my students, white or black. I acknowledged their tears and worked to use this emotional intensity to nurture awareness of our subject matter. Like every professor, especially females, I never want to cry in front of my students. As females, and in particular those of us who approach academic work from a feminist perspective, we are especially aware that sexist notions still abound that we are not the intellectual equals of males. One measure of our inferior status in the sexist mindset is the assumption that at times all females will be emotionally overwhelmed, that we will "come undone." Not wanting to reinforce this sexist thinking, almost all women professors would rather never shed a tear in the classroom.

Writer and activist Tillie Olson taught the first women's studies class I took as an undergraduate. Sometimes, in the midst of her poignant ramblings about the injustice of struggling with poverty, childbirth and unchosen motherhood, and an unkind husband, she would dissolve into tears. I must confess that I was rarely moved by her tears because they seemed to surface just at those moments when her "take" on women's lives was being critically questioned. I dubbed those tears a continuation of the "birth of a nation–white girl in distress tears" and saw them as sloppy sentiment. And of course in my undergraduate arrogance, I insisted (when students talked about these public displays of emotion among ourselves after class) that her tears had no place in the classroom; they distracted us from the reading and critical discussion. Black male writer and cultural critic James Baldwin once explained that "sentimentality is the ostentatious parading of excessive and spurious emotion…the mark of dishonesty, the inability to feel." This definition brilliantly describes the false sentiments that are evoked when tears are used to emotionally manipulate an audience.

As the lone black female student in many classrooms, I knew that voicing my disagreement with an individual white peer could lead to her crying and thereby becoming the center of attention, receiving sympathy from everyone else and drawing attention away from the issue of our disagreement. I knew that tears could be used as a weapon of distraction. I have been the target of a powerful rage that expresses itself through tears. When this emotional blackmail is taking place in the classroom, it, too, can be a teaching tool.

At City College in Harlem, I taught a seminar on James Baldwin with students who were incredibly diverse. One of the smartest and most engaged students in the class was a young, blonde white woman from Iceland. We were reading Baldwin's autobiographical writing in which he described being beaten harshly by his father. This led the class to discuss whether corporal punishment of children was acceptable. An older black woman, a single mother, declared: "I have a son and I have to beat him. He's got to learn or he'll end up dead on these mean streets, killed by some white policeman." A black male student spoke about how his mama would beat him with anything within reach—a broom, an iron, a lamp—stating that he would never forgive her.

In the midst of this intense discussion our young, blonde, blue eyed Nordic student, married and a mother of two, displayed a look of horror on her face, then burst into tears and ran out of the classroom. In that moment I had to make a choice, either to focus on her tears or to skillfully bring us back to the discussion of Baldwin's text integrating issues raised by the personal stories. I chose to do the latter. My choice was informed by the look of horror on her face; I felt it was crucial not to allow the negative judgment implied by her response to shift attention away from the matter at hand. I did not want to reinforce the assumption in this predominantly black classroom that white interpretation of black experience matters most. Then, as the discussion proceeded, I asked that someone find our missing class member and see if she had calmed down. When she returned to class, she explained to tough New Yorkers that in her country parents can be arrested for hitting their children. I made the assignment for the next class to write a one page paper exploring whether or not the terrible beatings Baldwin received had a positive or negative impact on his development as a writer.

Emotional awareness and the expression of emotions necessarily have a place in the classroom. Yet most teachers would rather there not be any crying or other intense displays of passionate feeling. Teachers simply have not been trained to know how to respond in a constructive manner when confronted by their students displaying overwhelming feelings. If we were trained to value emotional intelligence as part of being a teacher, we might be better equipped to make skillful use of emotions in the classroom.

It's not just students who bring their emotions into the classroom, so do teachers. Try as I might to never shed tears in the classroom, there are still times when I am just unable to repress them. Recently, I was teaching a group of students at the University of California, Santa Cruz where I studied years ago as a graduate student. One of my fellow graduate students, white and female, with whom I had many difficult disagreements, had gone on to become a professor who, like me focused on issues of race, gender, and class. Shortly before this teaching session, I had learned of her untimely death. Soon thereafter, I was standing in that Santa Cruz classroom more than twenty years later where the students had gathered to discuss my work. I began to talk about difficult dialogues, about the wonderful heady years of creating feminist theory as graduate students and I spoke about Ruth, the conflicts we had, the resolutions we came to do. My tears welled up until there was a great, emotional, tearful outburst as I wailed against her dying young, like so many other women critical thinkers. Bettina Aptheker, who had been a graduate student at the same time with us, was in the audience, and I could see that she was shedding tears, too. The students also had tears in their eyes.

It was clear that this utterly unplanned moment of emotional intensity was a moving lesson for the students that positive bonds rooted in respect and affection can emerge from relationships that began with much contestation and conflict. Before my lecture, the students had received a handout dictating the "correct" way to behave, instructing them not to interrupt, not to raise their voices. It read like a manifesto for "the repression of all dangerous emotions" in the classroom. I told the students that if we had abided by such rules when I was a graduate student then the critical discussions that laid the foundation for so much brilliant feminist theory to emerge would not have happened.

Writing about coping with breast cancer in her memoir *The Summer of Her Baldness*, artist and professor Catherine Lord poses this question: "Why, I wonder, is it unnerving to weep in front of a student…. Why is weeping in a classroom, though we have all felt like it, more of a threat to the mortar that holds together the bricks than stupidity or hatred or ignorance?" Weeping, crying, wailing, all displays of emotional intensity are feared in the classroom because they upset the hierarchy that would have us assume that the mind should always have dominion over the body and spirit. We are called to learn beyond the boundary of language, of words, where we share common understanding. We are called to learn from our senses, from our feeling states, and find their ways of knowing. If we allow for the possibility of tears, then an insurrection of subjugated knowledge may occur.

Teaching 15

Conflict

Feminist classrooms were the first places where I heard discussions about safety in the classroom setting. These discussions usually centered on the issue of students learning to talk together in ways that did not lead to conflict and hurt feelings. These discussions always annoyed me because I felt that they were more a reflection of the professor's fear that conflict would emerge and he or she would not be able to cope or that negative energy in the classroom would lead students to dislike the professor and the class; that to ensure good evaluations one had to ensure that students felt good. Ironically, in those classrooms much of what we had believed to be true about the nature of gender was being called into question. Belief systems that we had been comfortable with for all eighteen or more years of our lives were being contested. And yet we were being told that we should accept that this spirit of contestation and challenge should take place in a placid environment, wherein the rivers of our being should remain calm and no one should make waves.

Significantly, issues of safety became more of a concern in academic settings as classrooms became more diverse. This was especially the case when more black students/students of color entered institutions and classrooms that had previously been predominantly all-white. Racial difference was not the only factor creating a potentially tense situation. Since many students of color entering colleges for the first time came from poor and working-class backgrounds, class difference, perhaps even more so than race, estranged students from one another. In the race and class diverse classroom, students encountered experiences and perspectives different from their own. Initially, in some of these classrooms, students were often afraid to voice opinions for fear they might offend or alienate classmates, while in other classrooms, students were often overzealous in their efforts to confront and challenge one another.

Again and again I witnessed a communication breakdown in classroom settings when individuals who were speaking found not only that they had sharp differences of perspective but that attempting to engage in dialogue across these differences aroused intense passions, including anger and sadness. Tears and sorrow were easier for students and teachers to cope with than expressions of disagreement evoking covert and overt feelings of rage. The pressure to maintain a non-combative atmosphere, however, one in which everyone can feel safe, can actually work to silence discussion and/or completely eradicate the possibility of dialectical exchange.

Being both a dissident thinker and a militant feminist, I often find that I am challenged constantly by students who do not want to hear ways of thinking that are counter to conventional sexist thought. These students often seek to create conflict in the classroom that is destructive to learning, and that makes the formation of a learning community impossible. Managing this type of negative confrontation serves as a catalyst that pushes me to think in new ways about the issue of safety in the class-room. Instead of focusing on the commonly held assumption that we are safe when everyone agrees, when everyone has an equal time to speak, if we rather think of safety as knowing how to cope in situations of risk, then we open up the possibility that we can be safe even in situations where there is disagreement and even conflict.

Explaining this concept to professors in teaching workshops and to students in the classroom, I begin by talking about how we imagine a love relationship. None of us, irrespective of our sexual preference and/or practice, imagine that we can have an intimate relationship with a partner and always have seam-less harmony. Indeed, most of us assume that once the "honey-moon" period is over differences will emerge and conflicts will happen. Positively, we also assume that we will be "safe" in those moments; that even if voices are raised and emotions expressed are intense, there will not be and should not be any abuse or any reason to be unsafe, and that the will to connect and com-municate will prevail. Of course, most of us bring a greater will-ingness to trust each other in personal relationships than we bring to the classroom.

Yet, trust must be cultivated in the classroom if there is to be open dialectical exchange and positive dissent. It is helpful to explain to students from the start of a new class the importance of trust and the ways we link it to accountability. To trust means having confidence in one's own and another person's ability to take care, to be mindful of one another's well-being. Choosing to trust, to be mindful, requires then that we think carefully about what we say and how we say it, considering as well the impact of our words on fellow listeners. No true supporter of free speech endorses censorship, hence it is all the more important to be aware as teachers and students that our speech can be verbally abusive, that it can perpetuate domination and breed hate.

This awareness should lead to a profound appreciation of the privilege accorded us as citizens of this nation to be educated in a society where free speech and the right to dissent are core democratic values. It was a source of constant concern for me to witness students fearing to exercise their right to disagree or to engage in critical exchange. And it seemed especially disheartening when they were willing to forfeit the exercise of these privileges because they were concerned about what other students might think about them in the classroom and beyond. At times it was evident that students wanted to be liked by their peers more than they wanted to learn. These attitudes trivialize and undermine democratic education as the practice of freedom. Often, I would remind students that there are many places in the world where individuals fear that they will be imprisoned or risk their life if they speak freely. Fortunately, most of us, professors and students, do not face grave, life-threatening consequences if we speak out and engage in critical exchange. This is why it is of the utmost importance that we do not allow false notions of safety to interfere with creating a classroom community wherein students can learn how to engage in constructive dialogue, including discussion where there is intense disagreement. Unfortunately, it is often professors and not students who want to maintain the "safe" classroom because it is simply easier to demand that students cultivate an atmosphere of seamless harmony in the classroom and harder to teach them how to engage in meaningful critical dialogue.

When we teach our students that there is safety in learning to cope with conflict, with differences of thought and opinion, we prepare their minds for radical openness. We teach them that it is possible to learn in diverse teaching settings. And in the long run, by teaching students to value dissent and to treasure critical exchange, we prepare them to face reality. In the classroom and beyond they will face many situations where learning must take place in circumstances in which they may or may not feel in control, feel good, or feel that the mood will always be harmonious. True safety lies in knowing how to discern when one is in a situation that is risky but where there is no threat, and then again to be able to recognize when a situation, even a classroom situation, is unsafe and to respond accordingly. We choose risky situations everyday. Driving a car on any major highway places us at risk. But we all know that if we abide by the laws and cooperate with other drivers, we will increase the chances that we all reach our destinations safely. And the same holds true for classroom settings.

Teaching 16

Feminist Revolution

Within colleges and universities, feminist challenges to sexist thinking and sexist biases created one of the most amazing non-violent cultural revolutions our nation has ever known. Prior to the contemporary feminist liberation movement, the culture of our schooling was dominated by notions of learning rooted in the sexist assumption that females were not as capable of learning as males and that we had not contributed to ways of knowing. Such thinking informed the culture of schools on the primary level and on the university level. Education was used as a tool to reinforce the political system of patriarchy. As a consequence, a level of corrupt thought was disseminated in our culture of schooling that masqueraded as hard truth. The impact sexist thinking and biases had on ways of knowing created distortions and systematically supported misinformation and false assumptions, and thereby robbed learning of the integrity that should always be the foundation of knowledge acquisition.

Using education as a way to bolster patriarchal thought undermined democracy because it made education serve the concerns of a privileged constituency.

Long before there were organized contemporary movements to support equal rights for women, individual females and males had questioned and challenged sexism both in terms of what schooling taught and how folks were taught. The individual women who broke through sexist boundaries were beacon lights. Every male and female who witnessed their advancement was taught via their presence that gender equality could happen, that much that had been previously considered to be natural was in fact socially constructed. This was especially the case with individual academic women. The uniqueness of their circumstance always called attention to their working alongside men as equals, to their success. Consequently, their very presence was an intervention challenging and in rare cases changing sexist assumptions that sexism was "natural"; that females were inferior to males.

When contemporary feminist movement successfully challenged patriarchal assumptions that had heretofore informed every aspect of colleges and universities, a profound and necessary revolution occurred. The institutionalization of Women's Studies programs provided a sound academic foundation for scholars to interrogate sexist biases in the production of knowledge and provided a basis for corrective revision of previous bodies of thought. The feminist movement is subject to so much harsh critique that negative accounts of what the movement has accomplished (usually emphasized by patriarchal zealots) tend to overshadow the amazingly positive contribution feminist thinking and practice has made and continues to make toward redefining learning.

On a practical level, calling attention to the need to have job equity that would bring more women into the academic workforce was a demand that changed the face of academe. Even though the overall patriarchal structures underlying academic hierarchies remain intact, much of the way sexism over-determined the fate of females in the academy both as students and as teachers has changed. Anti-sexist advocates in the academy, both women and men, have not only worked for equal access, rewards, and representation, they have also fundamentally altered expectations in the classroom. The struggle to end the incorporation and domination of patriarchal knowledge in the academy has shifted so that, if nothing else, students can choose to study with professors who educate as the practice of freedom, whose perspective is no longer clouded by sexist thinking.

Significantly, the awesome impact of feminist thinking on higher education is most clearly registered by the constructive shifts (however relative) in curriculum and styles of teaching by those who still pledge allegiance to patriarchal thought and values. As our nation responded to the call for equal rights for women, the majority of our nation's institutions responded by making attempts to uphold gender justice, to be fair. Institutions of higher learning responded with the greatest willingness to unlearn sexist biases and to revise previously false information. Indeed, the revolution in education created by the widespread critique of sexism in conjunction with the overall feminist resistance to patriarchy on all fronts (social interaction, job equity, language use, curriculum material, etc.) represented a huge threat to the status quo. Organized anti-feminist backlash emerged to counter the positive impact of feminism on the academy. Conservative pundits attacked feminist professors, falsely insinuating that feminists were destroying the white male canon (clearly, no institution of higher learning in the nation stopped teaching courses that upheld white male canons), all the while insisting that feminists had created a tyranny of political correctness. In extreme cases, violent assaults on women in the academy increased as feminist challenges to sexism in and outside the classroom created widespread change in education.

Certainly, the intensity of anti-feminist backlash was a calculated response aimed at diffusing the transformative power of feminist thinking and practice in higher learning. It was especially threatening when individual academic men (most of them white) embraced a critique of patriarchy changing their thinking and their ways of teaching. Feminist thinking in the classroom brought an energy of opposition and dialectical exchange to the forefront in higher education. Even though the existence of a "feminist classroom" was rare (for such a classroom could exist only if everyone was engaged and committed to feminist thinking), without a doubt feminist theory and practice was a pedagogy of promise and possibility that was bringing new and powerful energy to the classroom. Feminist perspectives in the classroom affirmed the primacy of critical thinking, of linking education and social justice.

In the wake of anti-feminist backlash and a decline in the overall mass fervor of feminist movement, feminist perspectives tend to be embraced at most institutions of higher learning as simply yet another way of knowing. Recently, the critique of patriarchal canons, of imperialist white-supremacist capitalist patriarchal domination of academic thought has lost momentum, while a resurgence of overt anti-feminist thinking and patriarchal perspective has surfaced. Educators who recognize the importance of ending sexist biases that distort ways of knowing recognize the importance of maintaining feminist perspectives. Institutions of higher learning that would not allow female students to enter now have huge female enrollments. Major Ivy League schools that once denied female presence, now have female presidents who actively support feminist thinking.

No one would suggest that sexism in higher learning has been eradicated. Yet it would be impossible to deny the awesome changes feminist perspectives and anti-sexist activism have made possible in education. Educators must maintain critical vigilance to ensure that sexist biases do not once again become the norm. Feminist thinking restores integrity to higher learning and ensures that sexist biases no longer corrupt knowledge and the learning process.

Teaching 17

Black, Female, and Academic

Although our nation has made significant strides in the area of civil rights, the United States remains a society where racial segregation is the norm. The desegregation of schools was a landmark in the movement toward racial justice. And fifty or more years after Brown vs. the Board of Education, public schools in our nation are increasingly segregated by race and class. Surveys report that a large percentage of white Americans continue to believe the racist assumption that black people are academically and intellectually inferior. The persistence of racist thinking and action is the social backdrop undermining efforts to end discrimination in education on all levels. Large numbers of black students from various class backgrounds attended predominantly white colleges and universities in the wake of the civil rights movement, but that is no longer the case today. Since the public school system fails to educate a huge majority of black students from poor and working-class backgrounds, this group is ill-prepared to complete high school and will probably never seek higher education.

The fate of black teachers and professors is different from that of black students. Many of us teach in predominately white settings. Our classrooms are more often than not largely composed of white students. On the surface, it might appear that black professors would be accorded the respect and regard extended to any teacher irrespective of race. Yet a deeper look reveals that there are tensions and conflict that black professors (and other non-white professors) face that are vastly different from those of white colleagues. Black professors also face different issues based on our gender. While racist stereotypes have historically depicted black males as bestial and inferior, from slavery to the present day, there has never been a historical period in our nation where an individual black male has not excelled in academic study and been given recognition by white folks. The system of patriarchy ensures that the individual black females who excel, both in the past and in the present day, are rarely accorded the respect and attention their male colleagues receive.

Most folks probably assume that the working conditions black female professors face would not be so different from those of their black male counterparts. Since we live in a society that does not fully acknowledge the reality of race-based discrimination, while simultaneously denying the widespread prevalence of gender-based discrimination, there is a tendency to ignore the grave extent to which racialized sexism shapes and influences the way black females are perceived in daily life. Historically, one of the more common racist sexist stereotypes represented black females as bestial, overweight, jolly, mammy figures eager to serve and care for everybody. The mammy figure was often portrayed as being superstitious, full of folksy stories and anecdotes, wise in an intuitive non-self-reflexive way. She was not seen as smart or capable of academic studies. This stereotypical way of representing black females not only continued to be a part of racist sexist thinking once slavery ended, it gained greater currency as larger numbers of white women, from various classes, sought black domestic help.

Concurrently, when not represented as mammies black females tend to be viewed through the lenses of racist and sexist stereotypes as sexually loose, as sluts. Pornographic white male predatory lust for vulnerable black female flesh was the social context wherein this representation of black womanhood gained credence. To deflect attention away from their predatory sexual abuse of black females, white males insisted that black females were animals in heat, just waiting to pounce on any male in sight. The sexual devaluation of black womanhood, which began in slavery and continues into the present day, added fuel to racist sexist notions that black females were not capable of rational thought. A rare black female who excelled in academic work in the eighteenth and nineteenth century (for example, the poet Phyllis Wheatley) was looked upon as an exception, a freak of nature. With this historical backdrop, black females have had to consistently fight the stereotypes to gain any recognition of the power of our minds.

The one place where black females did not have to prove whether we were capable of excellence in academic study was in segregated black communities. There, black females were regarded as just as capable of learning as their black male counterparts, whether they were fortunate enough to receive an education or not. As segregated schools emerged, individual black females could aspire to become teachers. Once the work of teaching became a female dominated profession, more black women chose academic study. Certainly, growing up during the years of segregation, I attended schools where black female teachers set excellent standards for themselves and their pupils. Students who showed academic brilliance, whether male or female, were encouraged to develop themselves. There was no assumption that to study and learn in any way compromised black identity. Indeed, one's commitment to racial uplift was measured by academic striving. That has changed today. Internalized racism often leads black students to regard all teachers, but especially black female teachers, with disdain.

As racial segregation ended, black teachers and professors working in predominately white settings often found and find ourselves both the objects of abusive scrutiny and at times the targets of abusive harassment by both students and colleagues. In the classroom we often confront students who assume that "whiteness" entitles them to be seen as knowing more than the professor and therefore having the right to question and challenge in a manner that is disrespectful and disruptive. Because racialized sexism has socialized most white people, including students, to see black females as folks who should be subordinated caretakers, symbolic mammies, consciously or unconsciously asserting this unearned white privilege in the classroom is one way to reinscribe white supremacy.

To understand this dynamic fully, it is helpful to recognize the difference between white supremacy and racism. White supremacy underlies the assumption that black folks are intellectually inferior or not the equals of their white counterparts. But this does not necessarily mean that white folks who think this way seek to dominate black teachers from a position of racist discrimination. Many of my white academic colleagues express a longing to live and work in more diverse settings, to have black people as colleagues, but this does not mean that they have unlearned white-supremacist thinking. Most of the white students I have taught in more than thirty years of teaching have not exhibited overt prejudicial tendencies, racial hatred, or the desire to harm black people or people who are different from them. The difficulties arose and arise around unconsciously held beliefs and assumptions rooted in white supremacy (notions that black people are academically inferior, or that black people are racist if they critique whiteness and white privilege), which lead many white students to either constantly question the authority of a black teacher or to seek to undermine it. One of my sisters who teaches in public school shared that when a black female teacher was walking toward two white male students engaged in disruptive behavior one boy declared "We had better stop because the teacher is coming"; the response of the other body was that "Oh—she's just a black woman." Already this white boy who is still in grade school has learned to devalue black womanhood. Will he just suddenly learn respect for black female teachers when he enters college?

When I first began teaching, I learned from student evaluations that I was perceived as racist because I often called attention to racial identity: Any reference to white identity that linked it with the system of white supremacy created discomfort in the classroom. My critiques of systems of domination risked being viewed as expressions of personal anger. Again and again, black female professors come together and discuss among ourselves ways to challenge all students, but particularly those white students who wrongly project onto us that we are angry or mean. Individual black female professors complain that students see them as the "bitch" who is out to get them. Indeed, the idea for this essay began when a younger colleague asked me how we can correct and challenge white students without falling prey to racialized stereotypes that just lead to disrespect and a closing of the mind. She declared: "I'm tired of being seen as the angry mean black bitch."

Understanding that most of our students, irrespective of their race, have by virtue of being socialized in imperialist capitalist white-supremacist patriarchal culture internalized ways of thinking that are stereotypical, black female professors must enter the classroom prepared to challenge negative stereotypes when necessary. Very early on in my teaching career, in a course on black women writers, I was lecturing on Toni Morrison's *The Bluest Eye* and referenced the history of black women working as domestics in white households. A white female student raised her hand to disagree when I suggested that often black maids served white families with apparent good cheer and then

returned to segregated black communities venting their rage
and anger at ways they were exploited. The student kept repeatedly stating that their maid was a beloved member of the family,
who loved them as though they were her own. I questioned her
about whether she had ever talked with the maid about her
feelings, about race, about love, and her answer was no. I then
suggested that it was unlikely that she knew what the maid was
really feeling. The student cried. She accused me of being racist
and seeing racism everywhere. Taking time to clarify my positions deflected attention from the work at hand. And I learned
from this experience and many others that it was important
to talk about the issue of perspective, of biased and unbiased
thinking, to prepare students to hear points of view they might
not have heard before.

We must teach students to first see that perspectives vary de-
pending on the degree to which any of us have been socialized
to have blind spots in our thinking based on race, gender, and
class. Like the black female professors who talked with me about
the difficulties they face when they and their work are viewed
through the lens of racist sexist stereotypes, I find that negative
stereotypes projected onto black females often act as obstruc-
tions. Unenlightened students will often act out or behave in
ways that are aimed at forcing a black female professor to conform to their idea of who and what our identity should be; for
example, the professor who told me she had difficulty challenging her students without being seen as "a black bitch." Black
females are represented again and again in popular media as
angry, aggressive, and mean. All these traits are commonly seen
as evidence of being a "bitch." It is a constant effort for black
females in positions of authority to assert power while deflect-
ing negative projections that would deem all these assertions as
evidence of bitchiness.

Even though feminist thinking and practice focusing on
connections between racism and sexism helped generate
awareness of the way in which black womanhood is devalued in

an imperialist white-supremacist capitalist patriarchal culture, individual black females must continually work to challenge and change negative perceptions of our being and our behavior. As teachers, we struggle to resist students and colleagues placing us in the role of mammy caretaker because they have been unconsciously taught that this is a black woman's place. When I began writing and teaching about the connections between racism and sexism, I was often told that I was so angry. I refused to accept this projected identity. Instead, I would challenge audiences to consider why analysis of race, gender, and class that called into question accepted ways of thinking always appeared to them to come from a place of anger rather than a place of awareness. Often, the individuals who accused me of being angry were masking their own rage at being confronted and challenged. During the Obama presidential campaign, Michelle Obama was frequently portrayed as an "Angry Black Woman who resents white people, hates America, and may even have terrorist sympathies." Although there was no fact to document these assertions, they gained credibility because these are the negative misrepresentations of black female identity that have cultural currency. Concurrently, Condoleeza Rice, who emerged from the world of academic professorship to politics, was represented again and again as "unique and different" because she was so intelligent, as though she was an alien with no like counterparts.

Feminist movement coupled with civil rights efforts has compelled considerations of race and gender that enable black females to construct self and identity in ways that counter negative stereotypes. However, this does not mean that black female professors enter classrooms where racist and sexist ways of thinking and behaving no longer inform how we are regarded. Even though there are more black women receiving higher degrees and entering the ranks of professors than ever before in our nation's history, we are still likely to be seen as intruders in the academic world who do not really belong. Black female professors, especially those of us who are dissident, will never fully belong until racist and sexist biases no longer dominate our cultural consciousness. Until this change happens, any black female teacher or professor who challenges students and colleagues will need to find constructive ways to be assertive that intervene in all attempts to devalue our presence. It can be done. It does mean that black female professors who desire to have the greatest positive impact as teachers must work harder than other colleagues to create a learning community in the classroom.

Teaching 18

Learning Past the Hate

My favorite card game in childhood was Authors. Every card had a picture of a writer, and I never reflected on the fact that they were all white. They were not all male. My beloved Emily Dickinson was included. Each writer was important to me based on whether I found their work compelling. Dickinson was my very favorite and after her Emerson, Thoreau, and Hawthorne. Growing up in the segregated world of the South, attending what the white folks called "colored" schools, I did not associate race with learning. I did not know there was such a thing as a "canon" composed of the writers Western culture deemed "great." Every smart person in my world—every teacher—was black. They taught me the works of these writers whose words and ideas mattered so much to me in life. Finding an alternative sense of self and identity in the world of books as a girl, I did not think about race and writing.

In my teens I went in search of black writers. By then schools were integrated. Black children were bussed across town into a world of whiteness that did not want us—that had never included us. Determined to be a writer, I wanted to read the books written by black writers. White teachers, with no overt racist intentions, assured me that very few black folks had written books, and that what they had written was just not good enough to be read or taught in schools. Growing up in racial apartheid one learns a healthy skepticism in relationship to dominator culture. Black children were taught early on not to "trust" white people and their perspective on the world. They were not concerned with our well-being, with our intellect. Searching for black writers on my own, I found us: I found James Weldon Johnson, Langston Hughes, Georgia Douglas Johnson, and many more. I found a world of poetry written by black folks that was just as wonderful, just as compelling as the work of my beloved Emily Dickinson. The only canons I formed in my mind were filled with the writers with whom I felt a soul inspiring resonance, the writers whose works were great to me because they gave me words, wisdom, and visions powerful enough to transform me and my world.

Fortunately, I entered college just at the end of the sixties. A major revolution in education was beginning as radical and progressive thinkers had begun to question the extent to which racist and sexist biases shaped curriculum. Teachers were compelled to consider that their choices of what students would read and study were not politically neutral. In the academic world of literature studies, the traditionally exclusive focus on writing and thinking by white males who had been "deemed" great was being challenged. Teachers began to include writers who were not male, who were not white. In my first year of college, professors were still openly discussing and disagreeing about whether white women writers and black writers produced work that was "good" enough to be included. No matter a given professor's perspective, curriculum had changed and it seemed like there would be no turning back then. Civil rights movement and feminist movement had forever called into question white male hegemony. As the writers and thinkers we studied became more diverse, race and gender biases were interrogated. Aware students learned to stay away from those classes taught by professors who refused to consider the ways racism and sexism informed their choice of what to read and study.

At many liberal arts colleges, the professors who upheld dominator culture often found students fleeing their classes to study with teachers who were willing to be more inclusive. It did not matter whether the professors committed to inclusion were conservative or radical, what mattered was their refusal to make the classroom reinforce racist and sexist hierarchies. Successful curriculum changes that promoted inclusion and diversity threatened the existing status quo, and the upholders of imperialist white-supremacist capitalist patriarchal biases. The backlash began. Mass media was the propagandistic site for the dissemination of misinformation, telling the world that white male writers and thinkers were no longer being studied, that the classics in all fields were being ignored, and that "great" work was being displaced in favor of work by mediocre thinkers and writers. This was simply not true. However, a mass public was encouraged to see inclusion as a threat. Since this public had little or no contact with the ways courses are structured, they were an easy target for those who wanted to launch attacks on what was deemed the tyranny of the "politically correct."

In reality, the focus on diversity revitalized learning by changing education so that it would not reflect and uphold the biases inherent in imperialist white-supremacist capitalist patriarchal thinking. It returned an integrity to teaching and learning that had long been absent. In many cases, inclusion of new and different classes focusing on diverse thinkers and writers provided an invigorating boost to "traditional" departments that were experiencing low enrollment. Diversity in the classroom, both in the bodies present and in the subject matter studied, often created a constructive context for improved dialogue and engagement.

Despite all the misinformation circulated by conservative mass media, there really were no colleges and universities that displaced canons headed by a white male hegemony. No students who wanted to focus on a conventionally biased path of study were compelled to take courses that were aimed at increasing diversity and redressing biases. Women's Studies and Feminist Studies had been a central location for critiques of white male hegemony. Therefore, conservative pundits used mass media to suggest that advocates of feminism were teaching students to refuse to study white male thinkers and writers. In my entire teaching career, which spans more than thirty years, I have never heard a Women's Studies professor suggest that students should not study white male writers and thinkers. Instead, feminist thinkers encourage students to interrogate biases, and to think critically about male domination and the intersections of race and class. This true face of feminist thought has never been shown to the public by mass media.

Mass media seeks to simplify messages, so most of the complex academic issues involving diversity are never conveyed accurately or completely. Even progressive academics find it difficult to find or create an adequate language with which to discuss these issues. Certainly, in the study of literature many feminist scholars find it difficult to explain to students our conviction that it is important that they read works by authors who may be racist, sexist, engaged in class elitism, or homophobic. One of my favorite American authors is white male Southern writer William Faulkner. His works perpetuate both sexist and racist assumptions; however, this flaw in his vision does not mean that there are not many other redeeming features of his work. When I approach any writer who created during a historical moment when prejudicial thinking was more accepted, I approach their work from a standpoint that includes an awareness of multiple intentions. A writer may write to convey the specific beauty of a landscape and do that with astonishing, awe inspiring brilliance, but he or she may also express racist and sexist assumptions. If the work of that writer speaks to my soul in the way he or she uses language or describes that landscape my mind will choose to focus on the aspect of that work I find compelling.

My favorite Faulkner novel is *Light in August*. The title itself evokes memories of my Southern upbringing, of the way nature and light changes as the seasons begin to shift, the movement from summer into fall. There are, of course, many racist and sexist moments in this novel; Faulkner in that way was a man of his times. Yet in his transcendent vision he was a man who imagined way beyond the thinking of his times. This ability reminds us that when writers of any historical period use their work as a medium to express dominator culture, they are making a political choice. There is no historical period where we cannot find a thinker or a writer who dared to imagine beyond the constraints of the dominator culture of his or her time; they too were making a political choice.

On the one hand, Faulkner benefited greatly from his largely uncritical embrace of his unearned race, class, and gender privilege. On the other hand, he had a profound feeling of emotional connection to the subordinated, exploited black servants who cared for his well-being, both as a child and as a man. This is always the paradox inherent in any system of domination—that there is no "absolute" or closed system. Hence the ideology of racial apartheid could decree that whites and blacks in the American South should not be intimate and yet emotional connections happened. Bonds of intimacy and affection were forged. That intimacy and those feelings of mutual regard did not dismantle the system of racist domination, but no doubt the transgression of boundaries helped create the emotional climate that would later serve as a powerful context for Southern white folks engaged in civil rights struggle.

Still in my teens when I first read *Light in August*, I was deeply moved by Faulkner's fictive portrayal of Lena, the poor white female who dares to journey away from home. I learned lines

Lena spoke in the novel and quoted them as I went through life on my own journeys far away from the familiar, from the South, from home. I can barely recall moments of racist and sexist thought in the book. And it would have been a tremendous loss to my construction of self and identity if I had refused to read Faulkner because he was racist and sexist. Certainly, when I became a professor of American literature and taught his work I did not ignore or gloss over the prejudices and racial hatreds expressed by characters in his work but neither did I make that the central focus of our critical reading.

Perhaps no Southern thinker and writer has tutored my intellect as skillfully as white male Wendell Berry and yet I find his work to be at times quite sexist. Because I admire his work and have had the opportunity for fellowship with him in public and private, his ties to patriarchy sadden me for they serve as a barrier to our ever truly knowing one another intimately. Yet this knowledge does not alter all I continue to learn from reading and studying his work. He, too, is a man of his times when it comes to gender, but he radically resists domination in most forms that it takes in our nation. Since sexist thinking is a weak link, it would make all his work against domination stronger were he to be more progressive about gender. Even so, were his sexist thinking never to change, his work would still be enormously important.

When we have favorite writers and thinkers whose work we love and learn from, but who are still wedded to dominator thinking in any form, however relative, it disappoints. And that disappointment is always there in the shadows of our appreciation and our pleasure. When you are a member of a group that is disenfranchised, exploited, and/or oppressed you know intimately that any thinker or writer who supports dominator culture, even if they do so with the innocence of ignorance, supports a world that is wounding to you. It is not unlike being in a relationship with someone who is caring much of the time then occasionally abusive. In the long run, such a relationship diminishes. Black people have written very little about the impact on our psyches when we read work where the black characters are dehumanized. Surely, my enjoyment of *Huckleberry Finn* is never as complete as that of white readers. I cannot admire Huck wholeheartedly for there is no field of vision for me that does not include Jim. And I can never hear the phrase "nigger jim" without cringing. No doubt readers of any race or ethnicity who unlearn racism must find it equally difficult to unequivocally see Huck as a hero. Indeed, it is a question of politics and perspective.

At the college where I now teach, professors often choose a book for the entire first year class to read. The year I began my job I was given a copy of the book they were reading, a novel by a white woman focusing on coal mining and the struggle to create unions. It was assumed that the reading of this novel would help students better understand the political world of Appalachia. While the author had clearly worked to create a new role for white female characters, depicting them as feminist, radical, courageous, her portrayal of black characters followed a stereotypically racist script. White male characters expressed their racial hatred throughout the novel and the radical pro-union black male is brutally murdered. When I suggested to colleagues that it might be dispiriting for black Appalachian students, especially those who were among the first generation to attend college, to be bombarded fictively by such intensely negatively racist sentiments and portrayal, they responded with the usual insistence that the racism expressed by characters simply "was how it was back then." Of course I called attention to the fact that sexism and misogyny were expressed openly back then but the author seemed to think it was important to offer a more progressive image of white females. And again it must be stated that works of fiction are inherently not required to conform to actual fact or reality and usually they do not. Readers need to remain critical when characters voice intense prejudice and hatred of any group.

Certainly, I am more willing to read work from the past that includes stereotypically racist, sexist, and/or homophobic thinking when there is a larger context where the vision expressed is more expansive. Reading contemporary literature, I am less willing to embrace work that is violently prejudicial in its portrayal of any group. During my graduate student years I learned to think critically about race, class, gender, and sexuality. And I became fully conscious of the reality that it is almost always painful to be identified with a group that is portrayed in a stereotypically hateful manner, particularly by work that reinforces the hegemony of imperialist white-supremacist capitalist patriarchy. For example, if I am teaching a work of fiction which depicts a brutal rape, I recognize that anyone in the class who has been a rape victim will experience this writing differently and should proceed with caution. With no need to call attention to anyone, I can simply inform the class that there may be content in the work that could be disturbing or painful. Today, if I were teaching my beloved William Faulkner, I would take more time than I did twenty years ago to discuss the political context that was the background for his writing, not to diminish his work in any way, but rather to enable students to place in proper perspective his allegiance to dominator culture and his use of fiction to both perpetuate and interrogate those values.

Issues of diversity both inside and outside of the classroom once openly addressed are slowly being pushed back into the realm of silence and misinformation. As global oligarchy becomes the political norm, here and everywhere, we need education that addresses the world's diversity. More than ever before, students need to learn from unbiased perspectives, be they conservative or radical. More than ever before, students and teachers need to fully understand differences of nationality, race, sex, class, and sexuality if we are to create ways of knowing that reinforce education as the practice of freedom.

Teaching 19

Honoring Teachers

Among young school children we can see a reverence for teachers that soon disappears. Little children leaving home for the first time and coming to school learn that they must trust the teacher to care for their well-being as much as they trust parents. They are guided in this trust by parents who believe that their children can have faith in a teacher's positive intention because they share that faith. If it were not so, they would not be confident that teachers would care for their children wisely. Despite the value of showing respect and regard for teachers, by the time students are teens they will tend to regard teachers as negative authority figures or as outright enemies. It is impossible for education to take place within a context where a discipline-and-punish model frames social relations. When overt hierarchal power dynamics make domination of the weak by the strong acceptable, then students will not respect teachers and vice versa. They may indeed show deference, but the core of this trait is not respect but subordination.

Talking with teachers, especially those in public schools, I have heard their laments that the lack of respect for teachers begins in the home. Many of them talk about our present-day culture of narcissism and its impact on young people. They talk about the way in which many teenagers disrespect their parents, who indulge and pamper their children for fear of losing their affection. Sadly, there are those parents who have such a weak bond of attachment that they are threatened if the child shows attachment for a teacher. These parents worry that a teacher may have too much influence, so they encourage their child to disrespect the teacher. There are cases wherein a teacher is imparting knowledge that strengthens the self-actualization of a student but that growth is not promoted in the home.

Concurrently, many students, especially those in higher education, perceive education to be a commodity. They think of teachers as low level workers in the "factory" of knowledge, as service workers, like maids and janitors, whom they may have been taught to disregard and disrespect. Certainly, on campuses where students pay huge amounts of money for tuition there is an even greater tendency to see professors as workers who have less status than students, since the students see themselves (via their parents) as paying the wages of their teachers. Violence against teachers, both in public schools and in colleges, is often enacted as students endeavor to subordinate teachers. Fear of violence has made many teachers feel that it is best to remain aloof from students. They imagine that creating emotional distance between students and themselves will ensure that conflict will not emerge. However, if genuine closeness cannot emerge between teachers and students, the learning process is impaired.

In high school, individual students may genuinely like a teacher, seeing them as an important influence, but they may still show a lack of respect. Like their high school counterparts, college students may like particular professors and show them deference. However, that deference may be affected and expressed with the intent to be ingratiating. Usually, professors reveal that they hold a student in high regard prior to reciprocation from the student. This is a reflection of the unbalanced power arrangement. Students fear rejection; professors fear rejection as well, but usually our self-esteem is more intact.

Whenever a teacher, at all levels of learning from public school to higher education, befriends a student, there is a risk that the student will see this friendly resonance as a gesture that supersedes their hierarchic relationship, be it constructive or positive, which always accords the teacher greater authority. During my first years of teaching as an assistant professor at Yale University, I found it expedient to tell students when class first started that I might have great affection for them, but if they did not work hard or do required assignments that their grades would reflect the quality of their work. I decided to express this fact openly because early on in my teaching career a student for whom I felt much affection did poorly and was devastated when his grades reflected the lackadaisical nature of his class participation. He came to my office hours and repeatedly stated; "I thought you liked me." Sharing that I still liked him, I called attention to the way I would be doing him a disservice by rewarding him with a grade he did not deserve.

The assumption that affection dissolves the unequal nature of a teacher/student bond is one of the reasons it is difficult for students in our society to revere teachers. In any society governed by the politics of imperialist white-supremacist capitalist patriarchy, most relationships involving hierarchy will be structured using the model of domination. Explaining this model in her book *The Power of Partnership*, Riane Eisler writes: "In the domination model, somebody has to be on top and somebody has to be on the bottom. Those on top control those below them. People learn, starting in early childhood, to obey orders without question." Since many of our students think this way, they are often obedient and show much deference without feeling genuine regard.

A major transformation in education will happen in our culture when teachers on all levels receive deserved regard. When teachers are revered, admired profoundly and respectfully, our ability to teach is enhanced as is the ability of our students to learn. This is misunderstood often in Western societies where reverence is confused with subordination. To honor a teacher with reverence does not require subordination. In a democratic society where there is so much emphasis on equality, there is a tendency to forget that inequality does not necessarily mean domination is taking place. At the onset of feminist movement, many feminist professors were concerned that they not be dominators, dehumanizing students and asserting unjust power over them, so they strived to behave as though teacher and student were equals. This denial of the reality of hierarchy made it difficult for students to fully respect teachers and learn. It made the classroom a community without integrity.

We are not all equals in the classroom. Teachers have more power than students. And in dominator culture it is easy for teachers to misuse that power. Often students who have been raised in dominator thinking are uncomfortable with any teacher who repudiates this paradigm and seeks to create mutuality in the classroom. In the context of mutuality, a partnership can emerge between teacher and student. In this partnership, there can be affection and friendship at the same time that there can be deserved respect for the role of the teacher. Riane Eisler suggests that "the partnership model supports mutually respectful and caring relations," and that, most importantly, "power is exercised in ways that empower rather than disempower others." To achieve a greater sense of mutuality in the classroom, teachers must dare to teach students the importance of mutual respect and regard. We must be willing to acknowledge the hierarchy that is a real fact of our different status, while at the same time showing that difference in status need not lead to domination or any abuse of our power. When our society fully values teaching, it will incorporate rituals of regard that will teach everyone, especially students, to recognize and respect teachers. Individual professors who receive the respect and reverence of their students know how much this affirmation enhances our power to teach and increases our satisfaction with teaching.

Teaching 20

Teachers against Teaching

Believing that education is important to self-actualization and self-development, I make time to encourage folks who have either never tried college or dropped out without finishing degrees to come back to school. One of the most common explanations I hear for why they were not able to complete coursework is that the classes they were attending were just "too boring." When folks are asked to explain what constitutes a boring class, they usually lay blame on the professor. They do not think of the classroom and what happens there as created by the mutual interplay between professor and student. To them, the classroom "belongs" to the professor and she or he is the sole factor determining what takes place there. This is the way most students have been taught to think about education in the classroom. However, what takes place in the classroom is never simply determined by a professor, even one who may be boring.

During my undergraduate and graduate studies, I found

most of my professors were not compelling teachers. Many of them seemed boring because they were not at all enthused about the knowledge they were seeking to impart. In retrospect, I remember very little about those classes; mostly I recall the tedium. Majoring in English, I often found myself enthralled by the books on the course syllabus even when I did not find the classroom lecture and/or discussion interesting. When professors offer intriguing work to read and study it can serve as a basis for learning even if the classroom is not a compelling place. During my first years of teaching I did not want to be at all boring so I tried to devise teaching strategies to engage us all. Thinking critically about teaching during that time, I focused on the classroom as a learning community that required the mutual participation of teacher and student. Letting students know that they were participants in creating and sustaining a constructive classroom dynamic helped to lessen my initial sense that it was solely my responsibility to make the classroom an interesting learning place.

Nowadays, when a student comes to me to complain about how boring a professor is, my first response is to ask what they have contributed to the classroom dynamic. Clearly, professors have more power and indeed bear greater responsibility for what takes place in the classroom, but students also shape dynamics. Even if a professor is particularly dictatorial and chooses to be the primary speaker in a classroom, whether students are active or passive listeners will determine whether or not the energy in the classroom is positive or negative. Simply put, there are those occasions where a class taught by a boring and/ or non-communicative professor is made interesting because of student enthusiasm and engagement.

In his unpublished treatise *Learning Redefined* Professor Dennis Rader contends that "teaching is a leadership position." Yet many teachers may have no leadership ability, even if they truly love the subject matter they have chosen to study. Their handicaps as a teacher are made all the more crippling when students are taught compliance. Rader explains: "As we redefine learning we will look more closely at what is intellectually and emotionally nourishing for our students.... We should never teach for unthinking compliance. We should also not teach in ways that excite resentment and resistance." Just as the students' will to learn must be encouraged and nurtured, teachers need to learn effective ways to teach. A non-traditional student shared with me that she had taken a class where the professor talked at such a fast pace that most students could not follow his instructions, but no one gave him constructive feedback. Students complained among themselves, but they did not share with him the information that might have helped him become a better leader. Rader suggests that "as we understand the nature of learning we will forget all this training in methodologies and help teachers understand how to initiate and maintain conditions in their classrooms conducive to the emergence of learning—because the action of learning is emergent." Most teachers want to work effectively. Very few teachers want to be boring.

It is easier to assist a professor who is engaged with the subject matter but lacks communication skills and harder to intervene in the classroom when a professor seems to be both utterly disengaged and dehumanizing in her or his approach to students. One brilliant middle-aged over-forty black woman who made the decision to return to college and complete the last two years of undergraduate work found that the most difficult obstacle was the struggle to find meaning in classes where professors were simply disengaged. Often, professors who are considered terribly boring and/or disinterested teach courses students are required to take in order to graduate. Usually, these classes cannot be avoided. Mostly students do not learn in such a context; even when they are able to regurgitate assigned material, it is quickly forgotten when they leave the classroom. Sadly, professors who could care less whether they truly teach their students tend not to notice the ways their actions discourage and damage students.

Although it is not easy for students to challenge and change these circumstances, there are ways to try and improve the situation. The best intervention can happen when all the students in the classroom write a letter, one that may or may not be signed, sharing how they experience the classroom, stating what is not working while also sharing their positive intentions and hopes for the class. An individual professor who seems not to care may have arrived at his or her current state in response to students who seemed not to care. Of course, there are those cases where a teacher is wedded to dominator culture and, as a consequence, sees students as unworthy of regard. The only hope in such a situation is that students can find support and affirmation in their interactions with one another. In any classroom setting, it is vital that professors, like students, receive constructive critical feedback. A teacher who is unaware that he or she is behaving in a manner that is wounding or dehumanizing, when confronted is likely to alter the behavior. Teachers who use their position of authority to perpetuate systems of domination, whether it be racism, sexism, homophobia, class elitism, or unjust favoritism should be avoided. Even so, it is important to let them know, whether through face-to-face encounters or anonymous letter writing, how their actions wound and damage students. Now and then even the most mindful professor may unwittingly fail to give a student needed attention and regard. The student may leave the encounter diminished. Again, teachers cannot work to repair wounds if we are not made aware of when and why a student hurts.

Any student who comes to college with fragile self-esteem may be more easily wounded. Students from minority groups entering college for the first time may feel more at risk. They may respond to white professors who behave toward them in a dehumanizing manner by simply dropping out or failing. As education and learning are re-defined, I hope there will be teacher training that aims to help teachers better understand behavior that diminishes students and behavior that promotes learning.

Teaching 21

Self-Esteem

Despite the reality that most graduate students will seek teaching careers, there is little or no focus on training us to be teachers. The assumption seems to be that teachers who are preparing to teach at the public school level need training, but not the group which is being schooled to be professors. Given this reality it is not surprising that the issue of self-esteem is never raised as a concern all professors might need to address if they are to prepare us to be excellent teachers. There has always been an accepted notion that smart people have good self-esteem and therefore need not work at building it. In actuality, many "smart" children harbor deep feelings of low self-esteem and learn that academic achievement can be the best cover-up.

On a basic level, most people think that self-esteem means feeling good about oneself. Offering a broader understanding of self-esteem, psychotherapist Nathaniel Branden shares the insight that fully realized self-esteem is "the experience that we are appropriate to life and to the requirements of life." Explaining further, he states that

> self-esteem is confidence in our ability to think,
> confidence in our ability to cope with the basic challenges
> of life and confidence in our right to be successful and
> happy, the feeling of being worthy, deserving, entitled to
> assert our needs and wants, achieve our values, and enjoy
> the fruits of our efforts.

Given this definition, it is clear the development of self-esteem should begin early in life and be strengthened as an individual grows and matures. Indeed, public schools are one educational setting where issues of self-esteem are discussed, usually in reference to the needs of poor children from exploited and/ or oppressed disenfranchised groups. For many such children, school becomes the location where Branden suggests they are given a second chance, "an opportunity to acquire a better sense of self and a better vision of life than was offered in their home." Of course, it is a commonly held assumption in public school settings today that scarce resources and overcrowding of classrooms make the practice of teaching difficult. In such settings there is little room for the repair of wounded self-esteem.

Teaching in the university setting, I encounter students who are deeply wounded in their self-esteem. These wounds act as a serious obstacle to learning. They are present both in students who are underachievers, who may or may not come from exploited and/or oppressed groups, and possibly from dysfunctional families, and in students who may be quite confident of their intelligence but who may also be coming from dysfunctional homes where they were shamed and disrespected. In my earlier books on teaching, I shared the way in which the education I was offered in graduate school assaulted already fragile self-esteem. Professors who enjoyed shaming and humiliating specific students chosen to be the scapegoat were the norm in my experience. Usually they were male and, more often than not, white. The more they were deemed "brilliant" by their peers, the more they were allowed to dehumanize and violate students with impunity.

Often I lecture at small, exclusive, predominantly white liberal arts colleges where black students/students of color express intense rage at the racism of the institution and the racist practices of white professors. It has always led me to ponder why the so-called best and the brightest of these groups choose to come to "whiteness"' to be educated and then expend huge amounts of energy complaining about the omnipresence of whiteness. However, over the years as I have met with many of these students and listened to their stories, the core truth of their complaint is often not racism solely, but the way in which teachers have violated their spirits through disrespect and shaming. When you have grown up in schools where you have been "chosen" and at times celebrated for being smart, it is almost traumatic to then enter into institutions of higher learning where you may simply be ignored. In those locations you may still be the best and the brightest, but professors may show no interest in your academic responses or performances, thus rendering the student invisible. This practice of dehumanization is much more insidious than any full-frontal attack. Indeed, when individual professors used ridicule and sarcasm to attack my self-esteem, I usually responded with a sheltering and shielding rage. Protecting that rage often served as an obstruction that prevented me from experiencing joy in learning. Fortunately, I encountered a few of those rare teachers in my college career who offered me the opportunity to learn critical thinking, and who showed me how to be discerning.

A primary problem with self-esteem in the classroom is that a great majority of teachers lack this very crucial character trait. And while many teachers are smart in book learning, many come from dysfunctional family and school settings where independent thinking was discouraged and punished, where shaming, blaming, and verbal abuse was the norm. It is no wonder that our classrooms are often places where authoritarian values rule the day. Describing the context that produces the wounded inner child, therapist John Bradshaw concludes that shame-based family rules deny the five freedoms: "the power to perceive, to think and interpret, to feel, to want and choose; and the power to imagine." These rules are present in poisonous pedagogy. When students come to me with stories of how their humanity is assaulted by professors, especially those teacher-tyrants with whom they must take required classes, I urge them to see this unavoidable reality as practice for strengthening their self-esteem. If a student's lack of self-esteem is so grave that to be in such a classroom setting is life-threatening, they should be guided to appropriate help and necessary alternatives. I hope that as progressive pedagogy gains greater momentum, there will be avenues for those training to be teachers, whether in public school or college, to work on their wounded self-esteem.

While professors in colleges and universities continue to say little about self-esteem, those among us who care do hear the broken spirits of our students speak when they come to us behind closed doors, and, sadly, during those times when we visit them in hospitals and sick rooms, where they have tried to lay their shame to rest through suicide. At such times we feel the depths of their despairing lost sense of self. More often than not, professors deny the enormous power we wield in relation to a student's self-esteem. Teachers who acknowledge this power are far more likely to use it in the service of raising a student's consciousness so that they may realize their potential. It is the teacher who must first recognize the hidden treasure in the student with wounded self-esteem. Working to uncover that treasure is the mutual process that prepares the ground for a student to build healthy self-esteem.

I have witnessed the process of psychological growth in black students who learn to decolonize their minds, leaving behind the residue of racist indoctrination that gave them no firm ground on which to construct a positive sense of self and identity. In my early years of university teaching, I, too, was somewhat brainwashed and felt that my central role was to impart knowledge, that it was not my role to be a therapist. Yet it soon became apparent to me that if lack of self-esteem served as a barrier to students' learning, then I would have to help them to work at removing that barrier so that the information and knowledge I hoped to share could be constructively grasped by them.

I became accepting of the need to assist my students with their psychological growth when I began to see this work as enriching my teaching rather than diminishing it. This became all the more apparent to me when I encountered highly intelligent students performing poorly because of their low self-esteem. If I wanted to teach them, I had to address this issue. Certainly there are many "smart" students who manage to learn the game of storing information and spewing out facts when necessary, thus making it appear that healthy self-esteem is not essential to the learning process. Their flaws become apparent, however, as one follows these students throughout their years of study and on into teaching careers. They are more likely to be authoritarian, autocratic, unhappy in the classroom, sadistic toward students, or just plain mean.

Teachers can promote healthy self-esteem in students by showing appropriate appreciation and awareness of their potential. This does not mean that praise should be given indiscriminately. It does mean that calling attention to strengths a student may possess and encouraging her or him to work from that foundation can provide the necessary confidence that is the key to building healthy self-esteem. In my classrooms, I work to teach students how to evaluate their own progress so that they are not working to please me to get good grades. They are empowered by working in a manner where they recognize their responsibility and accountability for the grade they receive. That empowerment reinforces healthy self-esteem.

I hope in the future that all teachers will be trained to consider healthy self-esteem to be a crucial and necessary component of the learning process for teachers and students. When this awareness is commonplace, we will all have the opportunity to grow psychologically in ways that will make teaching and learning a place where working through problems, mutual respect, caring, and cooperation are the foundation of a meaningful education.

Teaching 22

The Joy of Reading

Even though I grew up in a working-class home as one of seven children in a patriarchal household where our father worked and our mother stayed home, my parents were readers. They believed in the power of books. And, naturally, they valued education as a means of social mobility. From early girlhood on I was encouraged to read. Even though Rosa Bell, my mother, had never graduated from high school, she bragged about her passion for reading and sought eagerly to share that passion with me. Against my father's wishes, she was willing to spend money on books, to let me know the pride of book ownership and the joy of possessing the gift that keeps on giving—the book that one can read over and over and over. I did not read silently to myself. I carted my books around the neighborhood to read to the elderly and shut-in, to share with them my treasures.

Like our young mother, our older daddy valued reading. He had graduated from high school and had received a license to be a barber, but instead he had chosen to do odd jobs, finally working for more than thirty years as a custodian at the post office. Our dad was a reader. The one bookcase in our house was filled with books he had chosen, the fancy set of encyclopedias, works by black authors, the classics of white Western Literature. My father, Veodis, was a race man; he believed that if black people wanted to improve their quality of life, we had to struggle to obtain civil rights and to educate ourselves. Like many of his contemporaries, he believed that learning to read and think critically about the world we live in was more important than a college education or college degrees.

In retrospect, I understand now the wisdom embedded in dad's assumption that it was more important to know how to read and think than to have formal schooling, especially given that current statistics state "the official estimate of illiterate American citizens now stands at 40 million." Quoting this figure in his insightful polemic *Gag Rule: On the Suppression of Dissent and the Stifling of Democracy*, Lewis Lapham comments:

> As many as six out of ten American adults have never
> read a book of any kind, and the bulletins from the
> nation's educational frontiers read like casualty reports
> from a lost war. The witnesses tell mournful stories about
> polls showing that one quarter of the adults interviewed
> were ignorant of the news that the earth revolves around
> the sun, about the majority of college freshmen (68
> percent) who have trouble finding California on a
> map....

I know firsthand the experience of teaching students who simply have little or no interest in reading. Professors who teach literature courses encounter reluctant and hostile readers in every course. My decision to stop teaching full-time was influenced by the apathy of many students about reading. And even though throughout my teaching career there have been amazing students who were utterly engaged with all material placed in front of them, the non-readers just simply began to be a toxic presence interrupting class discussion. It was always astounding when students who did not read assigned material wanted to hold forth verbally in class discussions.

Unlike most of my colleagues, I was able to find a place for my work in academe that allowed me to teach audiences of students, staff, and faculty who do read, who do want to engage with assigned material. Instead of full-time classroom teaching, I do short residences with intensive focus; in these sessions, readers read. Of course, there is much discussion about the role of technology, specifically about computers displacing books. Yet reading books on computers can never be the same as holding a book in one's hand, returning to pages without the aid of electricity or batteries, reading passages aloud to oneself or another person, reading the book in bed, lingering over pages, reading aloud. For many the book is vital to the practice of constantly re-reading, but more essentially it is necessary for genuine learning. Books invite us to imagine.

Most teachers recognize firsthand that while new technologies, especially computers, can be great ways of acquiring information, they can also actually assault the senses and dull the imagination if misused. Already studies are being conducted which indicate that young children who have advanced skill using computers are unable to be imaginative. No one who uses computers in an extensive ongoing way can doubt that the role we play at our keyboards is often a passive one. When I have commented with colleagues that I have difficulty spelling, they look at me as if I have lost my mind, exclaiming "don't you have spell check on your computer!" My insistence that I want to improve my vocabulary seems to them to be a waste of time. Certainly, reading works to bring new words into my life.

After more than thirty years of teaching courses that require intensive reading, I have come to accept that my father was correct in his assumption that being a critical reader was more important than having formal education and acquiring higher degrees. A huge majority of our population in the United States stop reading books after high school graduation, still more after they receive undergraduate degrees. Significantly, there was a time in our nation's history when purchasing a book (rather than checking it out from a public library) was usually a sign of being a member of an affluent class or that one was striving to move from a lower class position. Nowadays folks of all classes buy books. Indeed bookstores with cafes and comfortable armchairs make the printed word, magazines, newspapers, and books accessible to everyone. Even so, this world of abundant reading material has not created a culture where reading books is the "cool" thing to do. It has made it possible for more people to own a book, even to throw a book away. During my growing up years in the fifties, I can truthfully say that I never saw anyone throw books in the trash. On those rare occasions where a thrown-away book was discovered, it was saved. In these times of material excess all over our nation people put books in the trash, or just sit them on a sidewalk, New York style. Right now in our consumer culture books are as disposable a commodity as toilet paper. A culture that does not value the book as artifact will not value reading.

While it was certainly an important and positive intervention for talk show host Oprah Winfrey to use her media power to promote books and encourage reading, many of the titles featured on her show are among those books most frequently discarded. As the book has come to be seen as mere commodity, an object to be placed on display or a trendy purchase, fewer books are read. Frequently, I review a book with this simple phrase "most bought, least read book." I know of no studies which examine what motivates consumers to purchase books and not read them. There are folks who buy a book and never make the time to open it. Tired of seeing an unread unopened book purchase lying around, they get rid of it.

Most readers of books, especially teachers and librarians, do not foresee a time when books will not matter, when literacy will not be deemed both a right and necessity for responsible citizenship. Yet all over our nation libraries are being closed for lack of funds. Bookstores do not exist in every city and town in our nation. Already economic depression is changing the fate of the book. Independent bookstores and independent booksellers are shutting down all over the place because they cannot sell enough merchandise to survive economically in a climate of high rents and exorbitant real estate prices. When contemporary feminist movement was at its zenith, small women's bookstores opened up all over our nation. Today, the vast majority of those bookstores have closed.

Independent bookstores are one of the few places that offer public access to dissident material. Books that may not be in corporate bookstores because there is no huge demand for them find a place and a reader in the small independent bookstore. As those bookstores close their doors, it will be easier for discriminating librarians and corporate bookstore owners to ban books simply by not making them available. There need be no public announcement that certain books will not be on the shelves, as book ordering and book buying is a behind-the-scenes process. Indeed, it is possible, due to the growing gap between those who have economic privilege and those who do not, that there will come a time when only people with means will own books. Given this possibility it is all the more important that citizens work to maintain the public library; it is the institutional place where democratic education founded on literacy is most valued.

There is much discussion about the changing demographics of the United States, highlighting that white-skinned citizens will be a minority. This fact does not correlate with efforts to make it possible for newly born citizens of color, raised in homes where English may or may not be spoken, to be literate. Without literacy, these new populations are simply doomed to earning slave wages for a privileged class of enslavers who prefer their workers deaf and dumb. Recent studies on literacy reveal that black males are fast becoming one of the most illiterate groups in our society. Many incarcerated black males live most of their adult lives in prisons. In past times, prison has been a location where many black males discovered books and reading for the first time in their lives. Conservative forces in our nation want to deny all prisoners access to books, claiming that reading is a luxury and not a right. Depriving prisoners of the right to read is deemed deserved punishment. That anyone should wish to deny access to literacy in our nation threatens the future of democracy.

Whenever I am asked by audiences to give an account of my journey from small-town segregated black working-class experience to being a well-known intellectual, I highlight the significance of reading and the importance of public libraries. Reading allows every citizen of this nation and the world to assume civic responsibility. We cannot be proper stewards of our environment, caring for self and the world, without the ability to read. Teachers in every educational setting are the individuals who bear the greatest ethical and political responsibility for promoting the power of reading. For unlike other citizens it is an aspect of our job to promote learning. And there can be no book learning without literacy. Students who lack basic reading skill cannot learn to their full capacity. Nor does it do a student who is a skillful reader much good if he or she is allowed to devalue reading. As more and more students see learning solely as a means to gain economic success, the power and pleasure of reading may seem completely unimportant if they do not see a direct and immediate connection between reading and their career goals.

Now in his old age, almost ninety years, my father is still a reader. These days he must look through a huge magnifying lens to see the words on the page. These days reading for him is a slow and difficult process but it is still a way of knowing the world that is essential to the process of living, thinking, and dreaming. And more than anything literacy keeps him in touch with a world beyond himself; it offers the possibility of connection. This is the gift reading gave me as a child growing up working class in a small-town world with very rigid boundaries. Just as the bumper sticker says, "books are the gift that keeps on giving." Reading empowered me to journey to places with the mind and imagination. Reading expanded my consciousness. Laying the foundation for a passion for words and ideas, reading made the impossible possible.

Teaching 23

Intellectual Life

When I was growing up in our segregated black Southern culture, I knew early on that I wanted to be a writer. I knew that what I did not want to be was a teacher. The profession of teaching did not interest me because it seemed to require skills I did not have. It required one to be able to communicate well when talking to others, to be willing to nurture the needs of others, to be able to stand in front of groups of young people and talk, to be able to discipline and punish, and to be willing to judge others. The teachers I knew taught in public elementary school and high school. I did not know any college professors. I had never spent any time on a college campus. Truthfully, even though I was a good student, on the honor roll and so on, I did not give much thought to attending college while I was in high school. And I found that I did not have to think about it because other folk (my parents, teachers, guidance counselors) all stood ready to make decisions for me. In our patriarchal authoritarian environment of home, church, and school in the fifties no one wanted to know my desires. It was a given: smart girls were meant to grow up and become teachers. And smart black girls from poor, working-class backgrounds had two choices: cleaning other folks' houses or teaching school. While everyone knew that it was possible to escape these professions by falling in love and entering a traditional marriage where the little woman stayed home, this was the stuff of romantic fantasy. Most smart black girls, poor and working-class girls, living in the segregated South knew from high school that they were far more likely to become workers whether married or not. Few married women from poor backgrounds had the luxury of remaining at home.

Although I wanted to write books, I never saw that as an avenue to make money. When I graduated from high school, the world was just beginning to really awaken and listen to the voices of black women. I often imagine what my life would have been like had I not come of age during the heyday of civil rights and women's liberation. Both those amazing, profound revolutions shaped my destiny. Those movements for social justice made it possible for me to go to college, to be awarded scholarships and loans, and more importantly they made it possible for me to truly know that I could indeed become a writer. During my final undergraduate year and throughout graduate school I was drawn to intellectual work. Discovering a passion for working with ideas, for critical thinking, and theory I found a new path for myself. Once again it was anti-racist civil rights struggle and feminist movement which served as the locations where I channeled my desire to do intellectual work, to become a cultural critic.

I offer this background to affirm that there are powerful reasons an individual might choose to be an intellectual in an anti-intellectual society. Of course it has only been in the last thirty years that individual black females could lay claim to choosing intellectual life as their vocation. A central aspect of my academic career has been the production of feminist theory and cultural criticism. Believing that criticism, when it is most constructive, enhances and illuminates our understanding of the world, of a particular subject or text, I was not prepared for the feedback I received from students, colleagues, friends, and family that revealed not only that they saw the work of criticism as negative, as always and only attacking, but that they saw me, and other critics, as hostile people. I have even been told by highly intelligent colleagues that "criticism is satanic"—that it is the devil's work. Certainly, the work of deconstruction appears to have a potentially destructive element. Deconstructivist critics were and are able to take apart a subject or a text showing its various possible structures of interpretation and meaning, but the end result was not always to expand understanding.

When I realized that readers of my work often projected onto me a harsh and negative persona, I found myself wanting to withdraw, to return to working in solitude, which had been my lot before my work received public attention. It was difficult to hear folks describe me as harsh or mean. And it occurred to me that though I have wanted to serve as an example to students, especially to female and/or black students, showing them how swell it is to be a critical thinker and intellectual, many of them would not make that choice because they do not want to be disliked. Concurrently, the fact that there is little money to be made doing intellectual work is another discouraging factor. Overall, though, it is critical work that seems to be dangerous terrain for students. Time and time again, I have had to explain that there is a useful distinction to be made between critique that seeks to expand consciousness and harsh criticism that attacks or trashes.

When the subject matter a critic works with and the conclusions drawn from that work have direct consequences for how we live in the world, the critic is much more likely to be regarded negatively. This is especially the case when working with issues of race, gender, and sexuality. It is especially the case

when an aspect of one's critical work requires the interroga-
tion and even the dismantling of previously held assumptions.
Much of the recent work on the issue of changing thought and
behavior reminds everyone that such changes are usually re-
sisted, that most folk would rather stay with the status quo even
if to change would be an improvement. In my previous books
on teaching, I have confessed to feeling disappointed when students express dislike for me and my classes. Nowadays, though,
I can accept that when we share knowledge that requires listeners to shift their paradigms there is almost always a letting go
that is difficult and painful. I reached this understanding after
receiving much feedback from students who would share how
much they "hated me and my class" until they went out into the
work world and began to find the lessons learned in the class
useful. Similarly, many of us read a book when we are not yet
ready to receive the teaching it contains and dismiss it as irrel-
evant; then we find time passing and we pick up that very book
again only to find it offering needed insights that help us heal
and grow.

When I think about the question of why to choose an intellectual life in an anti-intellectual society, what immediately
comes to mind is the transformative impact of new ideas and
knowledge. In retrospect, when asked how I emerged from my
dysfunctional Christian conventional working-class home eager
to follow ideas and learn new truths, I always call attention to
the power of reading. In the repressive patriarchal home of my
growing up, one freedom that was afforded me (not without
continual threat of punishment) was the right to read. Through
books I learned that there were other ways to think and live in
the world than the ways I knew most intimately. Reading about
the diversity of human thought and life, I wanted to understand
more about the choices my family had made. This hunger for
understanding served as a tremendous catalyst pushing me to
pursue a life of the mind.

Words fail me when I try to explain the sheer joy that surfaces when I work with ideas and come up with new ways of see-ing and thinking about a particular subject. In *Either/Or* Søren Kierkegaard expresses this ecstatic feeling in a manner that resonates with me:

> If I were to wish for anything I should not wish for wealth
> and power, but for the passionate sense of what can
> be, for the eye, which, ever young and ardent, sees the
> possible. Pleasure disappoints, possibility never. And what
> wine is so sparkling, what so fragrant, what so intoxicating
> as possibility.

Much intellectual work embraces the art of the possible; it is like an archaeological process where one goes deep in search of truths that may constantly change as new information comes to light.

True intellectual work is done in solitude. It takes hours of thought, study, and reflection, then it takes time to write (an-other solitary activity.) Luckily for many individuals, this rigor-ous work with ideas is our right livelihood, our calling. Just as new ideas helped me transform my life, I have been especially lucky to receive feedback from students and from readers about the way my work has helped change their lives for the better. This is such a rewarding and inspiring experience. Truthfully, a life of the mind is one of those journeys in life that once begun affords one so much freedom to roam and explore that there is really no turning back.

Teaching 24

Writing Books for Children

Teaching outside classroom settings is one way to ensure that democratic education is accessible to everyone. It also affords a marvelous opportunity for teachers to hone communication skills different from those which may apply in the classroom setting. There are many ways to develop a place of learning outside the classroom. One direction my work has taken that has given me a different audience has been the writing of children books. I began writing children's books in response to parents, mostly black mothers, who shared with me that while my theory books helped young adults decolonize their minds they wanted me to write books for children that would also challenge racism and sexism.

I remember thinking each time a parent would raise the issue of writing for children that I was too serious, that I just did not understand how my mind would create work that children would enjoy. As with all my writing, I began to think and meditate about whether this was a direction my work should move into, and if the divine forces of the universe called me in that direction I would willingly go. One night before sleep I began to think about issues of self-esteem in black children, especially girls. I thought about growing up in a household with five sisters and how obsessed we all were with our hair, five girls all of whom had different hair textures. Our mother Rosa Bell was a traditional woman who felt that it was not healthy to begin using hot combs on the heads of little black girls (like lipstick and black dresses, that could be our choice later on), so she combed our natural hair. Combing and plaiting all those heads had to have its special day and its special time. Remembering this before sleep, the pleasure we all experienced when mama cared for our hair, I awakened in the middle of the night, and began writing all the words to my first book for children, *Happy To Be Nappy*.

Before I began seriously considering writing books for children I thought about all the children's books I had read, how most of the ones especially written for black children were extremely overtly didactic. To me they seemed unimaginative and not playful. I knew that I wanted to write books for children that would offer new paradigms, new ways of seeing and thinking about the world, while also being fun books that were pleasurable to read. Like much of my theory work on race, gender, and class which was often stimulated by personal experience, I remembered the tender language mama often used with her girls; she called us her "girlpie." And there began the first sentence of *Happy To Be Nappy*: "Girlpie hair smells clean and sweet, is soft like cotton, flower petal billow soft." "Wow!" I thought when writing this, "where did that line come from?" Oh! The power of the imagination. It afforded me a way to think outside the box, to imagine ways of talking and thinking positively, joyfully about black girls and our hair.

Certainly, within imperialist white-supremacist capitalist patriarchy, black girls and all black people are daily bombarded with negative representations of our bodies, our selves that are intended to socialize us to internalize racial self-hatred. It is no easy feat to create images that portray us as we are and as we want to be, resisting representation, images that counter negative stereotypes. Yet when we invent ourselves, when we move outside the box that stereotypes and confines us, it is wonderful, awesome. I know this from all the folk, the big and little people, who responded to *Happy To Be Nappy*, sharing their pleasure in a fun silly book, celebrating new and different ways of thinking and talking about ourselves.

Writing books for children not only brought me a different reading audience, it also brought me into public talks and conversations with children, providing me a space to teach outside the usual college classroom setting. I can still remember the joy I felt when a group of small black girls, beautiful of heart and spirit, came to meet me after a reading and talk, wanting me to sign their books. They all burst into giggles and exclaimed, "you said our hair is like flower petals." And it was just plain to see that this image had been transformative, that it had given them a new and different way to think about their bodies. Of course in attempting to write books to free children, I came face to face with the reality that many people are more comfortable with the familiar ways of seeing and thinking about our bodies, our selves even if those familiar ways are rooted in racist sexist stereotypes. To find those new ways of thinking and seeing that Malcolm X taught us we must seek, so that as he framed it, we would "see each other with new eyes," we must "change our own minds."

While *Happy To Be Nappy* was in production, another black woman, Carolivia Herron, was writing about the hair of a black girl. Her book *Nappy Hair* was filled with negative comments, folks mocking her little girl protagonist Brenda, shaming her about her hair. This book received national attention when black parents challenged a white teacher who was reading it to her class of black students. Wisely, these parents did not feel this was a progressive book. After being shamed and mocked, the young black girl represented as ugly and mean jumps for joy. This is of course the stuff of grown folks' fantasy. Children who are shamed and ridiculed do not spontaneously fall in love with themselves and jump for joy. Yet this book became a best-seller, reminding informed readers of how well colonized most folks are in their minds and imaginations. It is a great gift to write books that aim to decolonize. It has been especially difficult to write books for children wherein the central characters are male that are anti-patriarchal and non-sexist.

We live in a culture that in many ways is not child-loving. And as I have explained at great length in the adult books on masculinity I have written, ours is not a boy-loving culture. I wanted to write a book that would celebrate boys and embrace the wholeness of their emotional being, a book that would be fundamentally anti-patriarchal. The book that emerged was *Be Boy Buzz*. And even though this was not a book solely about or for black boys, the images represented were those of black boys. Everyone in our culture is encouraged to see books that have white images as still being books for and about everybody. But the moment a book has black images, it is more likely to be seen as being solely for and about black people. Throughout the marketing for *Be Boy Buzz* I had to continually explain to audiences that while the representations were of black boys (and that was an important intervention as there are so few books that centralize these images) it was and is a book about boys for all boys, for all readers, for all ages.

It was important to me that this book with representations of black boys should show the fullness of boy being. And as black boys are often portrayed in ways that limit and confine their bodies, their selves, it was radical to have black boys represent all boys. In the book there is a moment when the text tells us the boy is sitting all quiet and still. In the first set of illustrations there was no boy on that page. Chris Raschka, the illustrator, who is white and male, heard me when I expressed my concern that we needed the image of this black boy sitting and think-ing as there were other images of him jumping and playing. To counter the racist and sexist thinking that does not see black boys as needing solitude, quietness, time for reflection and con-templation, we needed to offer this image. We needed an im-age of the boy reading a book (as noted in an earlier chapter, black males are fast becoming the most illiterate group in our society). Chris made changes.

Reader response showed the vital and transformative impact of the text and images. Parents talked and wrote to me about how just seeing the image of the black boy reading worked as an intervention on two levels, celebrating boys reading and also celebrating black boys reading. Public talks with children about this book challenged me to find new language to talk with a dif-ferent set of listeners who were not college students. At the very first public talk about *Be Boy Buzz* with a diverse audience, an avid reader, a little white boy, asked the question: "What's the buzz?" Wow! I had to think quickly about my choice of words. We talked about the sound the bee buzzing makes. We made the sound. We talked about how it grabs our attention, creating the BUZZ. And this book was giving attention to celebrating boyhood, the boy who can exclaim "hold me close don't let me down," the *Be Boy Buzz*. Wow! I am just too lucky that those grown folks reading my books called on me to use my mind and imagination and write some books to free children.

Teaching 25

Spirituality

One of the benefits of teaching at a Christian college is that there can be open discussion about issues of spirituality. Even though many professors who teach at the college do not see themselves as Christian, they are usually open to students raising concerns about God in the classroom. Although he does not teach at a religious institution, Professor Dennis Rader sees conversations about God as an important teaching tool. He explains:

> Most of my students have a resonance with the concept of God. When classes begin I usually tell the students I see them as a gift from God. I tell them that their task is to unwrap the gift and my job as a teacher is to help you unwrap the present that is the gift of yourself.

Most professors I spoke with who believe in God consider it best to keep God talk out of the classroom because there are many students who are not believers who might feel silenced and/or excluded by such talk. Unless a class specifically focuses on religion, keeping the classroom free of particular affiliations and dogmas is important when working to create a learning community. Even at a Christian college, heavy handed discussions of particular religious dogma can silence discussion or create a hostile, argumentative atmosphere.

When I contemplate the question of whether there is a place for God in the classroom, I focus on the importance of spirituality in daily life. And as the classroom is a part of daily life, spirituality comes into the classroom with us. Religion and spirituality are not the same. In *Ethics for the New Millennium* the Dalai Lama makes useful distinctions between religion and spirituality:

> Religion I take to be concerned with faith in the claims
> to salvation of one faith tradition or another, an aspect
> of which is acceptance of some form of metaphysical or
> supernatural reality, including perhaps an idea of heaven
> or nirvana. Connected with this are religious teachings or
> dogma, ritual, prayer, and so on. Spirituality, I take to be
> concerned with those qualities of the human spirit—such
> as love and compassion, patience, tolerance, forgiveness,
> contentment, a sense of responsibility, a sense of
> harmony—which bring happiness to both self and others.

This definition of spirituality makes references to qualities that when brought into the classroom can help establish an atmosphere of trust that draws teacher and students closer together.

In *Teaching Community: A Pedagogy of Hope* I included a chapter on "Spiritual Matters in the Classroom" in which I discussed the fear many people have of spirituality in education. Quoting educator Parker Palmer from his work "The Grace of Great Things: Reclaiming the Sacred in Knowing, Teaching, and Learning" who urges teachers to transform education "so it will honor the needs of the spirit" I confessed my deep yearning as a college student to find ways to honor the spirit. As a teacher I seek to find ways to impart to students the strength that comes from cultivating an inner life, one that affirms the needs of the spirit. Palmer shares his conviction that education should be about more than gathering information or acquiring job credentials: "Education is about healing and wholeness. It is about empowerment, liberation, transcendence, about renewing the vitality of life. It is about finding and claiming ourselves and our place in the world." To honor the "sacred at the heart of knowing, teaching, and learning" teachers must have the courage to connect the inner work of becoming a self with the outer work of learning, showing the myriad ways that one can influence the other.

Inner growth is a process of learning where the individual cultivates a quietness of mind that allows heartfelt emotional awareness to become apparent. It is a way to bring our inner experience to the fore. In *The Heart of Learning,* educator Steven Glazer links the development of an inner sense of self to a sense of the sacred, which he believes is the ground of all learning. He explains:

> Sacredness is not understood within a particular religious
> framework but instead as growing out of two basic
> qualities of our experience: awareness and wholeness.
> Awareness is a natural self-manifesting quality; it is our
> ability to perceive, experience, and know…. Wholeness
> is inherent, seamless, [an] interdependent quality of the
> world. Through experiences of awareness and wholeness,
> we begin to establish the view of the sacred.

Critical thinking in the classroom is one way to cultivate greater awareness. It enables students to better recognize the interconnected nature of life and by so doing brings them face to face with the sacred. They find themselves capable of a conscious process of watchfulness that is mindful and aware.

Qualities of the human spirit, like those identified by the Dalai Lama, including compassion, patience, tolerance, forgiveness, and a sense of responsibility are all vital expressions of care that can lead to the formation of an atmosphere of learning that is truly awesome. These qualities lay the groundwork for self-determination when they are cultivated in the classroom and outside in other areas of life. Students who are self-determining assume responsibility for their learning and are able to engage the teacher as a facilitator. Understanding the inner life, they have a sense of what is sacred that emerges from their own process of self-realization. These are students who, with like minded teachers, bring spirituality into the classroom.

Unlike those teachers and students who may seek to talk openly about God in the classroom, those of us who consider spirituality important rarely feel a need to talk about spiritual matters. To most of us, spirituality is about practice, how we live in the world and how we relate to self and others. When we bring conscious mindfulness to work in the classroom we often have an ecstatic experience. Everything flows wonderfully and learning takes place for everyone. I know this is happening when students do not want class to end, when class discussion continues out into the hallways and into the dormitory and into the streets. At times like this I feel myself to be in the presence of the sacred. These moments are not common. They differ from those days where we have a "good" class. It is the collective learning taking place that produces the sensation of communal spirit. And the reason why such classes happen on one day and not on another (no matter how well prepared teachers and students may be) is just pure mystery. If we have not created a teaching community which acknowledges that spirit matters, then such moments never happen.

Spirituality belongs in the classroom because it is the seemingly magical force that allows for the radical openness that is needed for genuine academic and/or intellectual growth. As I concluded the chapter on spirituality in *Teaching Community*:

To me the classroom continues to be a place where paradise can be realized, a place of passion and possibility; a place where spirit matters, where all that we learn and all that we know leads us into greater connection, into greater understanding of life lived in community.

Teaching 26

Touch

Before words are spoken in the classroom, we come together as bodies. We read each other through the gaze. As teachers, we are the focal point of a collective gaze before words are spoken. Our students are looking at us and wondering what our bodies have to say about who we are and how we live in the world. We see our students, too, as embodied presence. Even though all the ways we are trained as teachers encourage us to act as though we are disembodied, the truth of our bodies speaks to us. Being comes from the body. And if we listen to our bodies inside the classroom and out we learn more ways to relate to one another. In *The Eros of Everyday Life* Susan Griffin shares this insight:

> There is an eros present at every meeting.... If human
> consciousness can be rejoined not only with the human
> body but with the body of earth, what seems incipient in
> the reunion is the recovery of meaning within existence

that will infuse every kind of meeting between self and
the universe, even in the most daily acts, with an eros, a
palpable love, that is also sacred.

The presence of eros in the classroom ushers in the sacred.

We are afraid to acknowledge the presence of physical bodies
in the classroom. For when these bodies of flesh enter, so does
eros, so does sexuality. And no one has instructed us, teacher
or student, about what we must do with eros in the classroom.
It is no wonder then that usually eros moves solely in the direction of sexuality, students who fantasize about engaging in sexual relations with professors and vice versa, students with mad
crushes coming to office hours full of lust and longing. When
the sensuality of eros in the classroom moves in the direction
of sexuality, it creates chaos and dissent. When talking with students about the ways class dynamics are altered when there is
obvious sexual flirtation between a teacher and student, or, if
the class is relatively small, when two students are engaged sexually and bring that energy wherever they go, the overwhelming response was that these dynamics disturb and undermine
the learning process. When a teacher is blatantly engaged in
a sexual flirtation with a particular student in the classroom, it
turns all the other students into voyeurs. It excludes them and
denies them a voice, since they have no say about what they are
observing. Overt displays of sexual play in the classroom have
no place, whether surfacing in teacher/student relationships
or between students. This does not mean that erotic energy
emerging as eros can be banished from classroom settings. For
wherever our bodies are, eros will also be present.

Eros fuels eroticism. In the essay "Good Sex: Passionate Pedagogy" included in *Teaching Community* I share that:

Passionate pedagogy in any setting is likely to spark
erotic energy. It cannot be policed or outlawed. This
erotic energy can be used in constructive ways both in

individual relationships and in the classroom setting. Just as it is important that we be vigilant in challenging abuses of power where the erotic becomes a terrain of exploitation, it is equally important to recognize that space where erotic interaction is enabling and positively transforming.

Because we are bodies in the classroom our libido is present, also. Yet what is often forgotten is that libido can be expressed as emotional and psychic energy that may be sexually generated. Eros as the passionate life instinct triggered by libido is what makes us able to experience the ecstatic in our bodies. The experience of learning can be intensified when a teacher is able to garner the energy of eros, whether because there are erotic feelings generated by physical connections in the classroom or by personalities. Imagine that a professor is "turned on" by having several extraordinary students in a class whose presence just ignites the learning passion of everyone; this is the energy that can make passionate pedagogy that positively impacts everyone.

Even if it is the sexual body that comes to mind most often when we speak of passion in the classroom, there is also the sensual body. And in that space, non-sexual touch can also be a way to communicate, to generate positive connections. Touch is a way to unite, to bring our bodies into communion. Touch can take the form of an embrace, a hug, a hand shake, a tap on the shoulder, or even simply a hand gently resting on an arm. Effective use of touch in the classroom creates a space of comfort beyond words. It may be a small intervention when words stated are particularly difficult or painful to hear. In the anthology *Embodied Love: Sensuality and Relationship As Feminist Values*, Paula Cooey's essay "Woman's Body, Language, and Value" shares that "the exercise of one's sense of touch is the exercise of one's nature to communicate." She offers the insight that "touch provides the possibility for freedom and change, both personal and social." In the classroom where there is always a hierarchy that places teachers in a higher position than students, touch can offer a place of mediation.

Mostly female professors shared with me that students often ask to be touched, usually to be given a hug. Often when an individual student is troubled and I offer them comforting words, I find them wanting a touch as much as, if not more than, words. Answering the question "why touch" in her essay, Cooey explains that "touch...communicates in a way that exceeds or transcends reduction to verbalization...when words fail, touch becomes a major expression of extreme feelings." Usually it is after class when students flock around me, either in the classroom or as we are walking toward another destination that touch happens. I might walk arm-in-arm with a student who is feeling the need for affirmation that she or he will be able to do necessary classwork. The touch that holds them communicates confidence in their ability to do what is needed.

A white female professor who teaches a course in African American literature found herself very aware of the body when working with black students. When individual students sought touch, she recognized that they were asking her to be more than just a white woman who makes use of black culture but to be one with them, to show her anti-racist sensibility by a willingness to touch. When she shared this experience with me, I thought of all the years in which racist apartheid re-affirmed its power by the refusal to allow touch across the boundaries of race. This colleague and I touch. During difficult academic moments, we often give that reassuring hug that lifts us up, that tells in a place beyond words that we will make it through, that we are not alone. Cooey sees touch as healing ritual: "Transformation from a negative to a positive relationship between body and value needs formal recognition as the birth of a new identity. Ritual allows this recognition to occur." In dominator culture where bodies are pitted against one another and made to stand in a place of difference that dehumanizes, touch can be an act of resistance.

Often I hear male professors who may observe my touching a student say, "Oh No! You are not going to get me in trouble." More recent emphasis on sexual harassment makes male professors aware that any touch of a student on their part could be easily misinterpreted. While everyone is more cautious about issues of sexual harassment, males fret more that their touch will be misunderstood because so many of them have been socialized in patriarchy to see touch as always and only sexual. Vital lessons in anti-sexist thinking and behavior could be taught to male professors on the issue of touch. Learning when a touch is sexual and when it is not could be one of the lessons in Touch 101. Individual students often ask male professors if they can give a hug, and at such moments it seems clear to these teachers that students are not asking for sex. They may be asking for healing touch.

Although I tend to touch students more than other professors do, I am not as comfortable with hugs as I would like to be. In exploring my own discomfort, especially when a student I may not like wants a hug, I recognize that this momentary relaxing of boundaries makes me feel vulnerable. In the moment of any embrace, short or long, we are made fully aware of our bodies, how the other smells, breathes, etc. This way of knowing calls for a different level of accountability. Touch can bring us closer, but it can also be coercive and therefore estranging. Understanding the ways touch can promote union is an important lesson for any teacher. We are accustomed to grade school teachers using touch in the classroom. We recognize its value as a force that strengthens. Tracing the role played by touch in all our efforts to teach is a vital place of study; we need to know more. Certainly, touch that is healing serves as a shield protecting us from the forms of violence that are all around us. To make a place for touch in the classroom is to resist the closing of our ways of knowing that take us beyond words and demand we listen to the body and know ourselves as flesh.

Teaching 27

To Love Again

Love in the classroom creates a foundation for learning that embraces and empowers everyone. I began to think about the relationship between the struggle to end domination and love in an effort to understand the elements that made for successful movements for social justice in the world. It was clear that the focus on a love ethic was a central factor in the movement's success. In *All About Love: New Visions* I defined love as a combination of care, commitment, knowledge, responsibility, respect, and trust. All these factors work interdependently. When these basic principles of love form the basis of teacher–student interaction, the mutual pursuit of knowledge creates the conditions for optimal learning.

Teachers, then, are learning while teaching, and students are learning and sharing knowledge. In *To Know as We Are Known: Education as a Spiritual Journey* Parker Palmer contends that "the origins of knowledge is love," declaring:

> The goal of a knowledge arising from life is the
> reunification and reconstruction of broken selves and
> worlds. A knowledge of compassion aims not at exploiting
> and manipulating creation but at reconciling the world
> to itself. The mind motivated by compassion reaches
> out to know as the heart reaches out to love. Hence, the
> act of knowing is an act of love, the act of entering and
> embracing the reality of the other, of allowing the other
> to enter and embrace our own. In such knowing we know
> and are known as members of one community....

Essentially, then, love's place in the classroom is assured when there is any passionate pursuit of knowledge. Such thinking counters the tenets of those critics who believe love has nothing to do with our ability to teach and learn. Cynical about love, they raise the question of whether or not love in the class is disruptive, as it may serve as a distraction and create a lack of objectivity.

Contrary to the notion that love in the classroom makes teachers less objective, when we teach with love we are better able to respond to the unique concerns of individual students, while simultaneously integrating those concerns into the classroom community. When teachers work to affirm the emotional well-being of students, we are doing the work of love. Colleagues have shared with me that they do not want to be placed in the role of "therapist"; they do not want to respond to emotional feeling in the classroom. If we refuse to make a place for emotional feelings in the classroom it does not change the reality that the presence of emotional energy over-determines the conditions where learning can occur.

Teachers are not therapists. However, there are times when conscious teaching—teaching with love—brings us the insight that we will not be able to have a meaningful experience in the classroom without reading the emotional climate of our students and attending to it. In some cases it may require that we become more emotionally aware of psychological conflicts within a student that are blocking her or his capacity to learn. It may then be appropriate to steer a student in the direction of therapeutic care. Often, a large number of students who enter our classrooms have had or are receiving some therapeutic care, which makes them more resistant to learning in circumstances where their emotional intelligence is ignored or devalued.

Sometimes professors are fearful of engaging students with love because they worry about being engulfed. They worry they will become too enmeshed in a student's dilemmas. This fear is keenly felt by anyone who is unable to establish appropriate boundaries. Most of us, teachers and students, have been raised with a misguided understanding of love. We have been taught that love makes us crazy, makes us blind and foolish, that it renders us unable to set healthy boundaries. Actually, when we teach with love we are far more likely to have an enhanced understanding of our students' capabilities and their limitations and this knowledge ensures appropriate boundaries will be present in the classroom. It also helps to promote an atmosphere of safety wherein mistakes can be made, wherein students can learn to take full responsibility for gauging their learning skills so that they are not teacher-dependent.

When we teach with love, combining care, commitment, knowledge, responsibility, respect, and trust, we are often able to enter the classroom and go straight to the heart of the matter. That means having the clarity to know what to do on any day to create the best climate for optimal learning. Teachers who are wedded to using the same teaching style every day, who fear any digression from the concrete lesson plan, miss the opportunity for full engagement in the learning process. They are far more likely to have an orderly classroom where students obey authority. They are far more likely to feel satisfied because they have presented all the information that they wanted to cover. And yet they are missing the most powerful experience we can offer students, which is the opportunity to be fully and compassionately engaged with learning.

Often teachers want to ignore emotional feeling in the classroom because they fear the conflict that may arise. Much as everyone likes to imagine that the college campus is a place without censorship, where free speech prevails and students are encouraged to engage in debate and dialectical exchange, the opposite is a more accurate portrait of what really takes place in college classrooms. More often than not, students are afraid to talk for fear they will alienate teachers and other students. They are usually terrified of disagreeing if they think it will lead to conflict. Even though none of us would ever imagine that we could have a romantic relationship with someone where there is never any conflict, students and sometimes teachers, especially in the diverse classroom, tend to see the presence of conflict as threatening to the continuance of critical exchange and as an indication that community is not possible where there are differences of thought and opinion.

Many of us have not witnessed critical exchanges in our families of origin where different viewpoints are expressed and conflicts resolved constructively. Instead, we bring to classroom settings our unresolved fears and anxieties. The loving classroom is one in which students are taught, both by the presence and practice of the teacher, that critical exchange can take place without diminishing anyone's spirit, that conflict can be resolved constructively. While teachers in their leadership are in the best position to create a climate of love in the classroom, students have the power to share their love of learning in a manner that can ignite sparks in a teacher who may be emotionally disengaged. No matter the direction from which love emerges in the classroom, it transforms.

All meaningful love relations empower each person engaged in the mutual practice of partnership. Love between teacher and student makes recognition possible; it offers a place where the intersection of academic striving meets the overall striving on all our parts to be psychologically whole. Education will change for the better in our nation when all teachers learn to love both outside and inside the classroom. While I approach every teaching experience with a general spirit of love, a relationship of love often flourishes between a particular student and myself, one that abides through time. Students I love most intimately never seem to leave my life. As they have grown and become teachers or entered other professions, they still call on me to teach, guide, and direct them. That our teaching relationship formed and shaped by love extends beyond our time in the classroom is an affirmation of love's power. When I asked one of my students, now a law professor, if my love of her created an atmosphere of favoritism in the classroom, she laughed. She stated: "Are you kidding? The more you loved us, the harder we had to work." There can be no love without justice.

Love in the classroom prepares teachers and students to open our minds and hearts. It is the foundation on which every learning community can be created. Teachers need not fear that practicing love in the classroom will lead to favoritism or competition between students. Love will always move us away from domination in all its forms. Love will always challenge and change us.

Teaching 28

Feminist Change

Love Connects. Love Heals. Let Love Rule. Give Love: Great phrases for Valentine's Day cards. I like to imagine them carved on the candied hearts of my childhood we passed around so earnestly as children. The message I remember most from back then, in red lettering on a pink heart, stated "be mine." The words of love listed above are all phrases I write on the title page of the three books that make up my love trilogy: *All About Love: New Visions; Salvation: Black People and Love;* and *Communion: The Female Search For Love.* And even though they make great presents for Valentine's Day, they all challenge our culture's obsession with romantic love and partnership. Most people confess that friendships, and not romantic bonds, are the place where they first begin to learn the art and practice of loving. Yet the moment I tell anyone I am writing about love, they assume the topic is romantic relationships. And that is even more so if I mention males and females. Again and again, I have to state that love is as important in relationships between fathers and daughters, sisters and brothers, and so on.

Romantic love always gets more attention because it is the love relationship that involves the greatest element of choice and yet the foundation of our thinking about love, our hope and dreams usually starts in childhood in our relationships with parents and siblings, with relatives, and then with friends. And it is usually when our romantic partnerships fail to provide the love our souls seek that we end up searching the past to find out why things are going wrong, why we can't find that somebody to love, why we cannot find the love that will last. Even though ours is a culture that obsesses about love, most folks still think that the yearning to love and be loved is a weakness. And whether female or male, when we talk openly about wanting love and not having it we are more likely to be pitied than admired.

No wonder then that contemporary feminist movement mocked the female search for love and made it seem that power was more important than love. To have equality with men, it was just assumed we would need to forget about love and get our minds and hearts stayed on freedom. All feminist bashing of love did was to turn lots of women off the movement. Often women came to power only to find that there was a lack of love, and that no amount of power satisfied without love. For many women, the knowledge of how much love matters has come in the years after thirty, at a time when we begin to contemplate the true meaning of love in our lives, not the old patriarchal notions of love but an understanding of love as the heart of individual self-realization. Now we know, as I emphatically state in *Communion*, that "no female can find freedom without first finding her way to love."

It seems especially crucial to talk about love in and outside the classroom from a feminist perspective at a time when many of our female students who are quite brilliant find themselves full of self-doubt and fear. They may be fretting over whether or not they will be seen as cool if they exercise their intelligence, or they may be wrestling with the age-old fear that being smart means they will be alone. To teach them, both by our theory and practice, women professors who are advocates of feminism must have the courage to let our lights shine, to let our capacity to love self and others be revealed for the strength and power it brings. Students are not inspired by women professors who are powerful in the classroom but painfully subordinated in their personal lives.

The female search for love has to begin with the work of self-love. That old saying that if you do not love yourself you cannot love others just happens to be true. We are obsessed with loving someone other than ourselves because it is apparently really difficult for females to love ourselves. As long as patriarchy remains in place, independent, powerful self-loving women will always "threaten" the status quo. No amount of equality in daily life has rid folks of the stereotypes about confident women. No wonder then that powerful self-loving women looking for life-long partners, whether male or female, still face a world that sees us as just a bit suspect. It is fine if we are dysfunctional in our emotional lives and powerful in our work lives; it is when we are fully functional and self-loving that our efforts to create intimate bonds become more complicated.

No wonder then that our culture is breeding a huge mass of young women who want to be powerful in the workforce, make lots of money, go way beyond where any male has gone before, thus proving females are not only the equals but maybe even the superiors of males, and who reaffirm their "femininity" in traditional ways by being an emotional mess. These babes like to think of themselves as power feminists but what they fear most is doing the work of self-love. Fully self-loving women expect love from partners, and when we want those partners to be male it becomes harder to find a soul mate. That's why I remind everyone in *Communion* that looking for love and looking for a man are two different things. Finding a loving man is still difficult work in the culture of patriarchy, not impossible, but definitely not easy. Lots of men have raised their consciousness to a level where they enjoy interacting with powerful women but for whom choosing a partner who is powerful still inspires fear.

Clearly, women have been subordinated in relationships forever and have not found that this brings joy or happiness. The best assurance that any woman will know love is that she loves herself and uses this love as the foundation for full self-realization. Choosing a circle of love to dance in, a circle that may be made up of lovers, ex-lovers, a partner, friends, and family, she is assured of having good company and of never being alone unless she wants to be. As I testify in *Communion:*

> Wise women who love know that no matter the strength
> of patriarchy, women must assume accountability for
> changing our lives in ways that empower, for choosing
> to love, and for learning through love ways to overcome
> all the barriers that exist to keep us from being fully self-
> realized.

Think of love as the most heroic and divine quest life calls us to pursue. And let that journey begin with the quest to be fully self-loving. It is only fitting that women, having come so far in demanding recognition of our humanity, our equality, our gifts, and daily reaping the benefits of this struggle, wisely call for a return to love.

Teaching 29

Moving Past Race and Gender

In these times of extreme anti-feminist backlash, of mounting fascism, and its concomitant support of war and all things that are like war, it is vital that we celebrate the strength of sustained feminist movement, of Women's Studies. Its very existence, its survival, its continued growth and development is a testament to the power of solidarity between progressive women and men, especially the solidarity of individual visionary black women who have had to work against the conservative history rooted in sexist biases that once were the absolute foundation of feminist education.

In the introduction to her book *We Are the Ones We Have Been Waiting For*, Alice Walker shares this insight:

> It is the worst of times because it feels as though the
> very earth is being stolen from us...: the land and air
> poisoned, the water polluted, the animals disappeared,
> humans degraded and misguided. War is everywhere. It

is the best of times because we have entered a period...
of great clarity as to cause and effect. A blessing when
we consider how much suffering human beings have
endured, in previous millennia, without a clue to its
cause.... Because we can now see into every crevice
of the globe and because we are free to explore
previously unexplored crevices in our own hearts and
minds, it is inevitable that everything we have needed
to comprehend in order to survive, everything we
have needed to understand in the most basic of ways
will be illuminated now.... We live in a time of global
enlightenment. This alone should make us shout for joy.

As feminist educators we can shout for joy. And yet we must
also arouse our collective will to continue freedom's struggle, to
continue to use our intellect and our imaginations to forge new
and liberatory ways of knowing, thinking, and being, to work
for change. We must revitalize our critical consciousness, to re-
kindle the seeds of militant radicalism that are the roots of every
Women's Studies and Feminist Studies program and Women's
Research Center in our nation. To do that, we must dare to make
feminist meetings both times to celebrate and times to expand
our consciousness. Let us honor the insight of Audre Lorde who
once asked all of us, in all our diversity and differences of race,
class, nationality, religion, sexual practice, to "re-member what is
dark and ancient and divine within ourselves that it may aid our
speaking, our dreaming, our way of life."

When we speak of the ancient dark divine the intent is not
to re-inscribe some folksy image of the all-knowing strong black
female. Our intent is not re-mammification or the evocation
of any racialized sexist thinking that would render exotic the
bodies and beings of black women by suggesting that we are
innately more in tune with the earth, more soulful, more nurturing, more caring, more ethical than other groups of women
or that we represent a feminine alternative to patriarchy. Patriarchy has no gender.

When we speak radically of the dark divine, the invitation is for each and every one of us to transcend race and gender, to move beyond categories, and into the interior spaces of our psyches to encounter there the ground of our being, the place of mystery, creativity, and possibility. For it is there that we can construct the mind that can resist, that can re-vision, that can create the maps that when followed will liberate us. To embrace the ancient dark divine is to engage the political and the spiritual; engaging the dark divine, we are all called to empathic identification with black females globally. We are called to see clearly that the fate of black females in the world is the mirror into which everyone can look and see all our destinies unfolding.

During the early stages of contemporary feminist movement it was common to talk about black women as experiencing double jeopardy because we were likely to be victimized by both sexism and racism. Then, as the movement progressed, class was added to this equation and a discussion of triple jeopardy ensued. In actuality, black females are assailed on all sides, on so many fronts that words like "double" or "triple jeopardy" are simply inadequate descriptions. We face exploitation and/or oppression. We face dehumanization from so many locations that the feminist strategies for our continued survival envisioned so far are nowhere near as complex and as clearly defined as they must be if we are to thrive.

For black females globally and here in our nation, these are dangerous times. To create lives of optimal well-being and, most fundamentally, just to survive, we require a feminist theory and practice that not only raises consciousness but offers new and different ways to think and be, activist strategies that can only be radical and/or revolutionary because there is no place in the existing structure of imperialist white-supremacist capitalist patriarchy where we are truly safe, individually or collectively. When we come together to celebrate, for some of us, those of us who were engaged with Women's Centers from the inception find that our shouts of joy also must make way for moments of mourning, of ritual remembrance.

For in this unsafe world, we have witnessed untimely loss, the deaths of so many powerful black female voices, writers, thinkers, activists, artists, and visionary feminists. And for some of us, colleges and universities were the place where we first gathered, met one another face to face, and made our voices heard, experienced our first taste of a solidarity so sweet, so soul-nurturing that we were, indeed, literally carried away, ecstatically transported by the power of silences broken, by the sound of our decolonized speech. This is what Audre Lorde describes in conversation with Adrienne Rich when she declares: "What understanding begins to do is to make knowledge available for use, and that's the urgency, that's the push, that's the drive." In those heady days we were learning how to do just that. We needed the Women's Center and Women's Studies then, and we need them now. Much vital feminist theory/black feminist theory emerged in conversations and debates in these locations.

In the early days of the feminist movement, Toni Cade Bambara was with us, a leftist, social commentator, writer, leader of a black feminist vanguard, and lover of blackness. It was her voice that told us in the anthology *The Black Woman* that we needed to:

> set up a comparative study of the woman's role...in all
> the third world nations; to examine the public school and
> blueprint some viable alternatives; to explore
> ourselves and set the record straight on the matriarch
> and the Evil Black Bitch; to delve into history and pay
> tribute to all [black female] warriors...; to outline work
> that has been done and remains to be done in the area
> of consumer education and cooperative economics;[and]
> that we needed to get into the whole area of sensuality
> and sex.

These are just some of the insights we must remember and use.

Wisely, Bambara was telling us that we would need to move

beyond simplistic categories like masculine and feminine because, as she explains,

> I have always found the either/or implicit in those
> definitions antithetical to what…revolution for self is
> all about—the whole person…that the usual notions of
> sexual differentiation in roles is an obstacle to political
> consciousness…that a revolutionary must be capable, of
> above all, total self-autonomy.

Bambara writes these words in 1970 and yet audiences and
other black women engaged in feminist theory and practice still
ask me, "Are you black first or a woman?" We know that when
we ask them what feminist thinkers do you read and study, the
answer is almost always "none." This is why archives are important and why the continual study of our work is crucial. This is
why it is important that work by visionary black thinkers be col-
lected in archives, ones that are, first and foremost, accessible
to those who are engaged in the process of decolonization.

We know how easily and how quickly our words are forgotten, our histories buried. We all know that students, even our
Women's Studies students, often show no hint of recognition
when we talk about the works of Pat Parker, Lorraine Hansberry,
Barbara Christian, Endesha Mae Holland, June Jordan, Octavia
Butler, and even Audre Lorde. We know that feminist thinker
Michelle Wallace has theorized the nature and substance of our
continued invisibility because she has lived with the fear of erasure. In *Invisibility Blues* she reminds us:

> I have come to see the difficulties black women writers
> encounter as structural and systemic…. Because black
> women are perceived as marginal to the production of
> knowledge, their judgment cannot be trusted…. As a
> consequence black women are not allowed (by themselves
> as well as by others) to make definitive statements about

the character of power, agency, and resistance within and beyond the black community. If and when they persist in doing so, the discouragement is great.

Wallace's insight is yet another reminder of why it is important that our papers be gathered, respected, used. As we all know, there are a small number of individual black women writers who have managed to engage in the insurrection of subjugated knowledge in such a way that our work is read more broadly, studied in classrooms, and quoted in a variety of texts (I place my writing among this work). Yet this inclusion does not ensure lasting presence, continued visibility, or sustained recognition.

On one hand, it is awesome that the critique of race and racism by women of color, many of us black women, brought to feminist movement fundamentally altered the nature of feminist theory. Yet we can still read celebrated theory by white women that builds on this work without any mention of the individual black women thinkers who laid the foundation. To resist this erasure, we must do all we can to document, to highlight, to study, to celebrate, and most importantly to create work that is cutting-edge, that breaks through silences and the different walls that have been erected to block our vision, of ourselves and of our futures.

Ironically, as more work by black women has received attention, much of that work has become more conservative, reformist, and not radical. We get gender without feminism. We are offered womanism as though it is the antidote to a powerful poison, that dangerous substance being feminism. When we connect Wallace's writing on invisibility with the constant demand Lorde makes in her work that silences be broken, then we claim our power to make ourselves visible because we have both a theory that enables us to understand what hems us in and a theory that conceptualizes our power to set ourselves and our words free. Lorde challenges us to not be trapped by fear. In *The Transformation of Silence* she declares:

We can learn to work and speak when we are afraid in
the same way we have learned to work and speak when
we are tired. For we have been socialized to respect fear
more than our own needs for language and definition,
and while we wait in silence for that finial luxury of
fearlessness, the weight of that silence will choke us...
there are many silences to be broken.

At times we want to be silent about how grave our circumstances are. We do not want to speak about how difficult it has
become for black females of all classes to garner support in all
areas of our lives. We want to be silent about how hard it is to
raise consciousness, to critique, challenge, and change sexism,
within and beyond black communities (particularly when the
forms of black community that once placed us in meaningful
solidarity with progressive black men are eroding daily). All
black females, irrespective of class positionality, know how difficult it is to constructively change our lives so that we can have
the necessary health and well-being to fuel revolutionary visions
of social change.

Significantly, Toni Bambara, Audre Lorde, and June Jordan
were all critical thinkers who dared to be militant, to speak when
silence would have afforded them greater comfort. They all
wrote about the need for black females to claim the space of becoming whole. Speaking openly of her commitment to feminist
movement in the essay "Where Is the Love," Jordan testifies:

I am a feminist, and what that means to me is much the
same as the meaning of the fact that I am Black: it means
that I must undertake to love myself and to respect myself
as though my very life depends upon self-love and self-
respect. It means that I must everlastingly seek to cleanse
myself of the hatred and contempt that surrounds and
permeates my identity.... It means that the achievement
of self-love and self-respect will require inordinate, hourly

vigilance, and that I am entering my soul into a struggle that will most certainly transform the experience of all the peoples of the earth, as no other movement can, in fact hope to claim: because the movement into self-love, self-respect, and self-determination is the movement now galvanizing the true, the unarguable majority of human beings everywhere.

It is essential to our struggle for self-determination that we speak of love, as love is the necessary foundation enabling us to survive the wars, the hardships, and the sickness and the dying with our spirits intact. It is love that allows us to survive whole.

When I began to write books on love for a more popular audience, I would often hear from readers that I was no longer as radical, as militant as I appeared to them to have been. To those who would limit and define black female intellect, imprison us in academies where our teaching cannot reach the masses of people who are seeking life-changing theory and practice, love has no meaning. Hence they will not understand that it is the most militant, most radical intervention anyone can make to not only speak of love, but to engage the practice of love. For love as the foundation of all social movements for self-determination is the only way we create a world that domination and dominator thinking cannot destroy. Anytime we do the work of love we are doing the work of ending domination.

We, black females globally, have a long history of struggling through brokenness, of enduring great pain, and yet holding on. This is still the history of victimhood. The history that visionary radical black women are making in our lives and in our work, here today, is not a history that begins with brokenness. It is a history that begins with the recognition that the work of love is our revolutionary starting point, that to love ourselves no matter our circumstance is already to stand in the place of victory.

Teaching 30

Talking Sex

During my younger years, everywhere I went someone would ask me about or tell me news of my sex life. I would often joke that if I was having as much sex as the gossips reported, I would be spending too much time lying down to sit upright and write anything. When asked whether I was straight or gay, I would share that I was a sex radical. As I approached the age of fifty, the curiosity about my sex life all but disappeared. The only folks who wanted to know if I was doing it, and with whom, were women like myself: middle aged, mostly professional, feminists, women who considered each other "hot." We are a small minority. After many years of self-chosen celibacy, I still see myself as a sex radical. In the introduction to *Public Sex: The Culture of Radical Sex*, Pat Califia explains that being a sex radical means "being defiant as well as deviant." Furthermore, she explains:

> It means being aware that there is something unsatisfying and dishonest about the way sex is talked about (or

hidden) in daily life. It also means questioning the way
our society assigns privilege based on adherence to its
moral code, and in fact makes every choice a matter
of morality. If you believe that these inequities can be
addressed only through extreme social change, then you
qualify as a sex radical.

With this definition in mind, Audre Lorde would certainly
qualify. She refused to be silent about her sexual practice. And
beyond her courageous ruminations about black lesbian sexuality, she invited us all to think about the "the erotic as power"
in her insightful essay "Uses of the Erotic." She does not write
much about sex in this essay. Yet it is often quoted in essays
by progressive thinkers writing about sexuality. Its significance
both when it was first published and now is that it gave women
permission to talk openly about erotic energy, to not allow that
energy to be "relegated to the bedroom alone." To Lorde, claiming the space of the erotic was an essential act of resistance, a
way to stand against dehumanization and domination. Confident of the power of the erotic as transgressive intervention,
she contends "in touch with the erotic, I became less willing to
accept powerlessness." Speaking more explicitly about sexuality
in an interview in the anthology *Against Masochism: A Radical
Feminist Analysis* she contends: "Even in play, to affirm that the
exertion of power over powerless is erotic, is empowering, is to
set the emotional and social stage for the continuation of that
relationship, politically, socially and economically." Lorde's insistence that we must encourage the eroticization of equality
remains for me an important insight—one that gives me much
to think about when I think about sex.

For sex is a danger zone. In sexual desire, in sexual acts there
is so much that is not equal. I want to render equality erotic even
as I also know that inequality need not lead to domination. In
her compelling book *Love Does No Harm: Sexual Ethics for the Rest*

of Us Marie Fortune asks, "What would happen if equality itself was an erotic experience?"

> The possibility of a relationship with someone who is equally strong, capable, self-confident, and clear seems most attractive if one is really interested in a relationship: that is, in spending time with someone in an experience of intimacy and trust. Such a relationship requires time, energy, conversation, and compromise.

Learning from Lorde, Fortune emphasizes the importance of choice, of being involved in a manner that allows one to "receive sexually and emotionally." Many feminist thinkers are unable to constructively theorize the uses of the erotic in a place where there is choice but no depth of emotional connection. The delightful anthology *Her Tongue on My Theory* by the artist collective Kiss and Tell makes the point that after all our feminist movement "society's hatred for sex is profound." They make the point that most folks in everyday life still see sex "not just gay sex, any sex as, suspect, obscene, perverse, dirty." Interrogating the feminist notion that sex should happen in a context of emotional connection, of relation love, they raise the question: "What's so bad about sex for its own sake? No one seems to think that they should only eat if they are in love."

If Lorde were present, I would want to hear her speak about the uses of the erotic in relation to sex. I would want to share with her the meaningful connection I make between her work on the erotic and Frank Browning's work in *A Queer Geography: Journeys Toward a Sexual Self*. Browning contends,

> By erotic, I mean all the powerful attractions we might have: for mentoring and being mentored, for unrealizable flirtation, for intellectual tripping, for sweaty mateship at play or at work, for spiritual ecstasy, for

being held in silent grief, for explosive mutual rage at a
common enemy, for the sublime love of friendship. Any
one of these loves can and do happen with women and
men in my life. Any one of these loves—rage, ecstasy,
mateship—can drift into each other further complicating
and entangling our lives, leaving us to realize on parting
that the one with whom we feel the most powerful love
may be neither the one we most respect nor the one for
whom we feel the greatest lust. If I tell you first that I am
gay, our love will move in one direction. If first I tell you
that I love you—as a mate, as a comrade, as a spiritual
voyager—you will know my queerness in quite another
way.

Browning extends Lorde's vision to invite us to question notions of sexual identity. His expansive vision is one that does not
yet have a label. "Sex radical" might work, perhaps "queer" or,
as I often claim as sexual identity, "queer past gay."

Attempting to theorize sexuality, to talk about the erotic
and about sex in a liberating way created profound spaces of
silence within feminist movement. It is impossible to confront
these silences and not evoke Lorde's challenge that we break
silence—that we speak. In moving with and beyond Lorde we
need to speak a vision of mutuality in the space of the erotic;
in sex, one that does not require equality as a condition for
pleasure, for sustained passion and emotional growth. To eroti-
cize risk and danger is not to embrace domination. The erotic,
particularly in the realm of the sexual, can lead to spiritual and
emotional self-actualization, even if the place where it begins,
where desire places us, is imperfect, unequal, and, yes, potentially dangerous.

Teaching 31

Teaching as Prophetic Vocation

The more I teach, the more I learn that teaching is a prophetic vocation. It demands of us allegiance to integrity of vision and belief in the face of those who would either seek to silence, censor, or discredit our words. In Jim Wallis's book *The Soul of Politics* he maintains that the prophetic vocations require us to be "bold in telling the truth and ready to uphold an alternative vision—one that enables people to imagine new possibilities." The prophetic dimension of teaching is the least recognized in our nation.

Usually when I am asked what I do by shopkeepers, taxi drivers, bank tellers, or random folks standing in a line, I tell them I am an English teacher. To almost everyone, the English teacher matters. They are the teachers students most often remember, whether the memories are good or bad. And as adults no longer in school, when English teachers are mentioned, profound memories are evoked. It may be memories of how hard it was to read or write. It may be the remembered embarrassment of having to read aloud in front of one's peers. It may be memories of red marks on paper, lines drawn through words, or exclamation points. Sometimes it is just the memory of the English teacher writing "Yes," and affirming that we were understood when we felt uncertain. Or the memories may be more profound. We may remember when we began learning critical consciousness for the first time. We may remember the moment when we first learned to be existentially self-reflective. Or it may be simply remembering the reading of that first book that reached inside, pulling our heart strings until we felt the story, and our being was utterly transformed.

My favorite high school English teacher is long dead. Yet what I hold in my heart's memory about her is that she, and her classes, challenged me. She challenged me to think, to be and become, to create. Growing up in the midst of racial apartheid, right at that moment when desegregation was changing all our lives, when we black children were sent out of our familiar neighborhoods into a strange dominating white world to be educated primarily by white teachers, many of whom regarded us with hatred and contempt, black students considered ourselves fortunate to be in a classroom with a teacher who loved justice, who believed we were all capable of excellence. In such a classroom, we had the opportunity to learn.

My favorite English teacher, white and middle-aged, was seen as a "nigger lover" because she repudiated the racism and white supremacy of the world around us, because she wanted her classroom to be a place where black students could learn with as much passion and zeal as white students. I regret that I cannot talk face to face with her and hear her story of how she came to be a teacher willing to educate as the practice of freedom in the face of apartheid, of racial ignorance and racist brutality. I remember her warmth, her daring, her will to challenge. I remember that she cared for black students, affirming our wholeness and the rightness of our being. And most importantly, she did not shame us.

Shaming is one of the most common strategies used by educators in classrooms where prejudices prevail. Shaming dehumanizes. In Michelle Paige's essay "Going Beyond the Book," published in the issue "All Together Now: Embracing Our Diversity" of the National Council of Teachers of English's journal *Voices from the Middle*, she shares this powerful insight:

> We, as teachers, are called upon to be advocates
> for our students, to empower our students to be
> productive citizens, and to take full advantage of their
> rights. Teachers often see firsthand the detrimental
> efforts of structural and society inequality on students
> —particularly students of color. One way we can be in
> relationship with students is to work on their behalf and
> to teach them how to work against injustice as well.

The most vital, the most liberating strategy, that beloved teachers offered me, especially the English teachers who taught me, was learning to be a critical thinker: to ask questions, to reserve judgment while putting together the who, what, when, where, why, and how. When I am asked to talk about how I became "bell hooks," renowned writer and intellectual, I talk about the significance of critical thinking and how it helped me survive the racist, sexist, class elitism outside the home of my growing up and the dysfunction which sanctioned abuse, betrayal, and abandonment within the patriarchal home.

When students ask me what I most want from them, I share with them that my intent is not to make them become "little bell hooks." They need not think as I do. My hope is that by learning to think critically they will be self-actualizing and self-determining. Just as I recall with tribute and praise the English teachers who encouraged me to be an active learner, to embrace radical openness, I hope my students will look back and remember that I taught them to look for what is significant, to develop their intellects by working with ideas.

Teaching 32

Practical Wisdom

One of the most nurturing and generous benefits that comes when we engage in critical thinking is an intensification of mindful awareness which heightens our capacity to live fully and well. When we make a commitment to become critical thinkers, we are already making a choice that places us in opposition to any system of education or culture that would have us be passive recipients of ways of knowing. As critical thinkers we are to think for ourselves and be able to take action on behalf of ourselves. This insistence on self-responsibility is vital practical wisdom.

The vital link between critical thinking and practical wisdom is the insistence on the interdependent nature of theory and fact coupled with the awareness that knowledge cannot be separated from experience. And ultimately there is the awareness that knowledge rooted in experience shapes what we value and as a consequence how we know what we know as well as how we use what we know.

When we create a world where there is union between theory and practice we can freely engage with ideas. Our thoughts then are not abstract meaningless currency, of use solely to those who seek to live their thinking lives in an academic environment removed from the ways and workings of everyday life. In my life becoming a critical thinker helped me survive the traumas encountered in our patriarchal dysfunctional family setting. Seeking to know and understand fully gave me a way to create whole pictures in my mind's eye, pictures that were not simply formed through reaction to circumstances beyond my control. Understanding the larger frame helped cultivate in me the seeds of mindful awareness and compassion.

All too often the public assumes that intellectuals (who are by the nature of our chosen vocation critical thinkers) are dispassionate folk, all mind and no heart. The true intellectual, who always finds the courage to seek the truth beyond ego or fixed notions of the nature of things, is always walking a compassionate path. Buddhist teacher Thich Nhat Hanh writes: "Compassion is not an idea or something we can imagine. It is a mental formation that has an immediate result in action of body, speech, or mind. It is rooted in understanding." From a spiritual standpoint the practice of compassion creates empathy for others, an understanding of the circumstances that influence and inform their thoughts and behavior. From an academic standpoint looking at a more holistic picture, whether we are engaging ideas or communicating with colleagues and students, intensifies awareness and makes connection possible. Skillful connection and resonance enhances our ability to teach and learn.

As exemplified by our joy in ideas and our willingness to remain students—always lifelong learners—as critical thinkers, intellectuals are radically open minded. And when the mind is fully open, fully aware, we necessarily find ourselves understanding even that which we seek. For all true intellectuals are at heart lovers of truth. This does not mean that intellectuals cannot be corrupted by the will to gain power and prestige that surpasses that which is accorded most critical thinkers. When knowledge is used to dominate others it is always a perversion of intellectual pursuit. Clearly there are intellectuals and/or academics who are conservative, who identify with the dominant relations of power; however, this does not mean that they necessarily subordinate their passion for ideas to those values. Perhaps we would be able to change the overall anti-intellectualism of our society if the public were aware both through their own learning process and through positive contact with academics and/or intellectuals that ideas, theories, all ways of knowing can be used to help us live more fully.

Most teachers are not intellectuals. There are many teachers who are not critical thinkers. Importantly, one need not be either intellectual or academic to engage in critical thinking. Everyone engages in thinking in everyday life. There are many circumstances faced by ordinary folk that require them to examine reality beyond the surface, so that they can see the deep structure. These circumstances may lead them to ponder the question of who, what, where, when, how, and why and thereby start on the path of critical thought. When we accept that everyone has the ability to use the power of mind and integrate thinking and practice we acknowledge that critical thinking is a profoundly democratic way of knowing. Inviting us to critically examine our world, our lives, practical wisdom shows us that all genuine learning requires of us a constant open approach, a willingness to engage invention and reinvention, so that we might discover those places of radical transparency where knowledge can empower. Educator Paulo Freire consistently maintained that approaching knowledge in this way we develop "a permanently critical attitude." Learning to reflect, to broaden our vision so that we can see the whole picture is a basic tenet of practical wisdom.

Certainly, one element of practical wisdom that comes with critical thinking that is mindful and aware is the ongoing experience of wonder. The ability to be awed, excited, and inspired by ideas is a practice that radically opens the mind. Excited about learning, ecstatic about thoughts and ideas, as teachers and students we have the opportunity to use knowledge in ways that positively transform the world we live in. Enthusiasm for lifelong learning is promoted by critical thinking. Embedded in this understanding is the practiced wisdom that helps us remember that ideas are not fixed and static but always subject to change. Hence there is the capacity of ideas to illuminate and heighten our sense of wonder, our recognition of the power of mystery.

Concurrently, it is practical wisdom that leads us to recognize the vital role played by intuition and other forms of emotional intelligence in creating a fertile context for the ongoing pursuit of knowledge. Uniting knowledge gleaned from facts and hard data with social skills is a pragmatic approach to learning. Effectively using knowledge in and outside the classroom we develop an organic relationship to critical thinking and use the resources it brings in every sphere of our lives.

Index